THE BIG BOOK OF
VISUAL
SUDOKU

273 Puzzles That Reinvent the World's
Most Popular Number Game

BY MAKI KAJI
AND THE SUDOKU CREATORS AT NIKOLI PUBLISHING

Martha

WORKMAN PUBLISHING | NEW YORK

C🕐NTENTS

Copyright © 2011 by Nikoli Co., Ltd.

Design copyright © by Workman Publishing

Library of Congress Cataloging-in-Publication Data

Kaji, Maki.

The big book of visual sudoku : 284 puzzles that reinvent the world's most popular number game / by Maki Kaji. – 1st ed.

p. cm.

ISBN 978-0-7611-6579-8 (alk. paper)

1. Sudoku. I. Title.

GV1507.S83K35 2011

793.74–dc23

2011024198

Design by John Passineau with David Matt

Back cover photo by Akimitsu Hirosawa
Photo (page iii) by Hiromi Nagamoto

Workman books are available at special discounts when purchased in bulk for premiums and sales promotions as well as for fund-raising or educational use. Special editions or book excerpts also can be created to specification. For details, contact the Special Sales Director at the address below, or send an e-mail to specialmarkets@workman.com.

Workman Publishing Company, Inc.
225 Varick Street
New York, NY 10014-4381

www.workman.com

Printed in the United States of America

First printing September 2011

10 9 8 7 6 5 4 3 2 1

INTRODUCTION

Welcome to *The Big Book of Visual Sudoku*! Ever since we discovered this puzzle more than twenty-five years ago, we have been absorbed in the never-ending task of creating smart and elegant puzzles. But during the time we have been making new puzzles, we continue to nurture and develop Sudoku. We continue to think more about the solving process than about the end result. So it is with great excitement that we introduce to you *Visual Sudoku*, a reinvention of the simple game that offers a new challenge during the solving process. The same rules of traditional Sudoku apply, but this Sudoku is all dressed up and ready to play. And despite its attempts to go incognito, you'll still recognize the game you know and love, because if you peel back the visual layers, it is at its heart a puzzle handmade by the editors at Nikoli.

    The editors at Nikoli have a long tradition of crafting all Sudoku puzzles by hand—we believe it is the best way to create Sudoku, because it offers the best experience to the solver. In Japan, every bit of feedback from our solvers is considered as we constantly work to refine Sudoku in subtle ways (or innovate in more obvious ways—keep flipping through the pages of this book and you'll see!)—and that commitment, I believe, is one of the reasons why Japanese solvers prefer Sudoku by Nikoli. You may come across a program that can create Sudoku puzzles quickly, but it will never create Nikoli's Sudoku puzzles. I hope you'll enjoy that difference as you solve our puzzles in these pages—the sense of communication between solver and author, and that feeling that you're matching wits with a master each time you approach a grid. The best Sudoku puzzles make you concentrate, but aren't stressful. This doesn't mean that a good Sudoku must be easy. A human sensibility is required for fiendish puzzles, too!

*—MAKI KAJI, the "Godfather of
Sudoku" and the president
of Nikoli*

▶ WHAT IS VISUAL SUDOKU?

W e all know by now that Sudoku is a classic grid-based number game, a simple and perfect exercise in logic. Each puzzle is made up of 81 squares (called cells), which form 9 columns, 9 rows, and 9 boxes—each of which is a 3 x 3 square set off by a bold line.

1	2	3	4	5	6	7	8	9
4	5	6						
7	8	9						
2								
5								
8								
3								
6								
9								

In Visual Sudoku, we've replaced the standard Arabic numerals in the black-and-white grid with more colorful representations: The nine positions on a baseball field are highlighted in "Swing for the Fence!"; the first nine elements in the periodic table replace the standard digits in "The Elements of Style"; in "Carpe Sudokum" and "All Hail Braille," the puzzles have been translated into Roman or Braille numerals. And so on. The visual translations add an extra level of challenge to the game for a more whole brain exercise (a workout for the right side!). It's Sudoku in costume, Sudoku with a twist, Sudoku in vivid vibrant color—in short, it's Sudoku gone wild! Here's an introduction to each new puzzle variation along with tips for solving.

ROCK AROUND THE CLOCK

In this variation, clock faces replace the numbers. The time indicated by the hands on the clock face corresponds with the number in the cell (3 o'clock equals the number 3 in the grid, 5 o'clock equals number 5, and so on). Draw in the hour and minute hands to indicate the appropriate time on the blank clock faces in the grid. (Hint: The minute hand should always point to 12.)

CARPE SUDOKUM

I	II	III	IV	V	VI	VII	VIII	IX
1	2	3	4	5	6	7	8	9

A standard translation, this puzzle replaces Arabic numerals with Roman numerals. To solve, draw the correct Roman numeral into each blank cell.

ALL HAIL BRAILLE

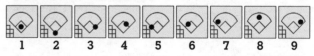

Though these are a visual representation of a very tactile written language, the dots on the grid here accurately represent the raised dots that make up a Braille character. To solve, color in the blank dots to draw the correct Braille character on each blank cell.

GETTING OLD SCHOOLED

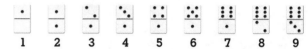

Glagolitic numerals are part of the oldest known Slavic alphabet, dating back to the 14th century (the numbers correspond to the order of the letters). In this puzzle, each symbol represents a number 1 through 9; to solve, mark the correct symbol in each blank cell.

THE DOMINO EFFECT

In this variation, an extra element has been added to the challenge: The solver must add together the dots on the two sides of the domino tile in order to determine the number represented in the Sudoku puzzle cell. To solve, draw the appropriate dots on the blank dominoes.

WHAT'S YOUR SIGN?

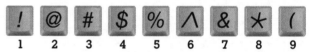

Nimble fingers articulate the first nine digits here. To solve, simply write the Arabic numeral into the blank cells to complete the puzzle (unless, of course, you're a talented sketch artist and prefer drawing hands!).

JUST MY TYPE

In this variation, the symbols on the number keys on a computer (or typewriter) keyboard represent the numbers 1 through 9. Fill the blank cells with the correct symbol to complete the puzzle.

THE ELEMENTS OF STYLE

1.0079	4.0026	6.941	9.0122	10.811	12.011	14.007	15.999	18.998
H	He	Li	Be	B	C	N	O	F
HYDROGEN	HELIUM	LITHIUM	BERYLLIUM	BORON	CARBON	NITROGEN	OXYGEN	FLUORINE
1	2	3	4	5	6	7	8	9

In this variation, the first nine elements on the Periodic Table of the Elements represent the numbers 1 through 9. Fill in the appropriate elemental shorthand in each blank cell to solve the puzzle.

SWING FOR THE FENCE!

There are nine positions on a baseball field, each represented by a number on the scorecard (pitcher is 1, catcher is 2, first base is 3, and so on). Mark a dot that represents the correct fielding position in each blank cell.

SPEED DIAL

The numbers 1 through 9 have corresponding symbols on the keys on a touchtone phone. (The number 1 has no symbols on the keypad, so the asterisk and pound sign have been combined to represent 1.) To solve, mark the correct combination of symbols in each blank cell.

PLAYING WITH A FULL DECK

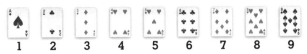

In this variation, the first nine playing cards in a standard deck (Ace through 9) represent the nine digits in the Sudoku grid. To solve, fill in the blank cards in each cell with the appropriate playing card number (drawing in the suit and color of each card is optional).

CAST OF CHARACTERS

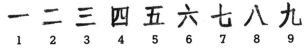

With this variation, we celebrate the Japanese origins of modern Sudoku. Traditional Japanese (and Chinese) numeric characters replace the Arabic numerals here. Learn the characters as you write them into the blank cells in the grid to solve the puzzle.

SUDO-KUBE

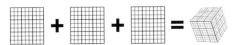

In this puzzle, it's a three-for-one. The brain gets a break from the symbols, but the eyes are treated to a colorful 3-dimensional puzzle. The puzzles don't interact across the edges, so you can solve each of the three puzzles separately, as you would a standard Sudoku puzzle.

▶ THE RULES OF VISUAL SUDOKU

As mentioned earlier, despite the change in appearance, the same basic rules of traditional Sudoku apply to Visual Sudoku.

1. Place a number or symbol (representing 1 through 9) in each blank cell.

2. Each row, column, and 3 x 3 box must contain numbers or symbols representing 1 through 9 without repeating.

▶ SOLVING METHODS

As with standard Sudoku, the level of difficulty (marked Easy, Medium, or Hard) depends on how many numbers or symbols are initially revealed, which also affects the technique you should use in approaching each puzzle. But the logic, as always, is based on the narrowing of possibilities. If you need a refresher, or would simply like to hone your solving skills, here are some basic patterns and techniques (expressed in standard Arabic numerals) to explore as you solve the puzzles.

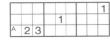

BASIC PATTERN 1

Start at the box on the left. The top two rows cannot contain the number 1 because of the 1s in the middle and right boxes. Therefore, the only place for a 1 in the first box is cell A.

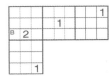

BASIC PATTERN 2

Basic Pattern 2 is similar to Pattern 1. In the upper left box, the top two rows cannot contain the number 1. The cell to the right of the number 2 cannot contain the number 1 either because of the 1 in column three in the box below. Therefore, a 1 must be placed in cell B.

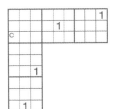

BASIC PATTERN 3

After learning Basic Patterns 1 and 2, it is easy to determine that the number 1 must be placed in cell C since it is the only cell in the upper left box that will not cause a duplication of 1s in either rows one and two or columns three and four.

BASIC PATTERN 4

In this pattern, the middle row in the upper left box cannot contain the number 1 because of the 1 in the box on the right. And the middle column can't contain the number 1 because of the 1 in the box below. A 1 must be placed in cell D.

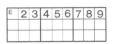

BASIC PATTERN 5

This pattern is easy: On the top row, E is the only cell remaining in which one can place the number 1.

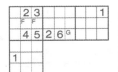

ADVANCED PATTERN 1

In the upper left box, the number 1 will be placed in one of the F cells because the 1 in the bottom box negates the possibility of placing the 1 in the first column. In the second box, the top row cannot contain the number 1 because a 1 already appears in the top row. The middle row cannot contain a 1 because one of the F cells will contain a 1. So, in the second box, the number 1 can only be placed in cell G.

ADVANCED PATTERN 2

To determine where the number 1 should go in the far right box, first look at the far left box. Because of the number 1 already in the top row of the box, a 1 cannot be placed in the entire top row. In the middle box, with the cells in the bottom row already filled with the numbers 2, 3, and 4, there is no other place for the number 1 than in one of the H cells in the middle row. So, with a 1 in the top row, and the necessity of a 1 in one of the H cells, the only remaining option in the far right box is to place the number 1 in cell J.

ADVANCED PATTERN 3

In the upper left box, the number 1 should be placed in either of the K cells. (Now no other cells in the top row may contain the number 1.) In the upper right box, the top and middle rows cannot contain a 1; its far left column cannot contain a 1 because of the cell that contains a 1 in the box below. Therefore, the number 1 must be placed in cell L.

ADVANCED PATTERN 4

Numbers 1 and 9 are missing from the top row. Because of the 1 already in the lower left box, cell M must contain the number 1 and the cell to its right will contain the number 9.

ADVANCED PATTERN 5

Numbers 1, 8, and 9 are missing from the top row. Cell N cannot contain an 8 or a 9 because they already appear in the left column in the lower left box. Therefore, the number 1 must be placed in cell N.

MASTER PATTERN 1

In the upper left box, the numbers 2 and 3 will be placed in each of the two P cells because the appearance of 2 and 3 in the left column in the lower left box and the top row in the middle box negates any other possibility. The number 1 cannot be placed in the top or bottom rows in the upper left box because of the 1s that appear in the top and bottom rows in the middle and far right boxes. Therefore, in the upper left box, the number 1 must be placed in cell Q.

MASTER PATTERN 2

Cell R cannot contain the numbers 2, 3, or 4 because they already appear in the same box. It cannot contain the numbers 5, 6, or 7 because they already appear in the same row. It cannot be the numbers 8 or 9 because they already appear in the same column. Therefore, cell R must contain the number 1. (This deduction may seem simple, but it's easily missed!)

THE HISTORY OF SUDOKU

The editors of Nikoli, Japan's leading puzzle company, discovered "Number Place" in an American magazine in the 1970s, and brought it to Japanese readers in 1984. (This puzzle was a variation on Latin Squares, developed in the eighteenth century by the Swiss mathematician Leonhard Euler. He had been inspired by an older puzzle called Magic Squares, which in turn can be traced to Lo Shu, an ancient Chinese puzzle.) Maki Kaji and his editors originally called the puzzle "Suuji wa dokushin ni kagiru," which means, loosely, "it is best for the number to be single." That title was not only too long but also confusing, so they abbreviated it to "Sudoku"—*su* meaning number and *doku* meaning single.

Sudoku didn't catch on at first, but in 1986, Nikoli introduced two new significant rules: First, all the numbers must be arranged in a symmetrical pattern, and second, no more than thirty numbers can be revealed at the start of the puzzle. The result was magical, and Sudoku became a huge hit.

AN INCOMPLETE HISTORY OF SUDOKU

Ancient China	1700s, Switzerland	1970s, United States	1984, Japan	1986, Japan
Lo Shu and *Magic Squares* are developed.	*Latin Squares* is developed by mathematician Leonhard Euler.	*Number Place*, often credited to Howard Garns, an Indianapolis architect, appears in an American magazine.	Nikoli gives *Sudoku* its name and introduces the puzzle to Japanese readers.	Nikoli introduces two new rules to the game of *Sudoku*—the result is magical.

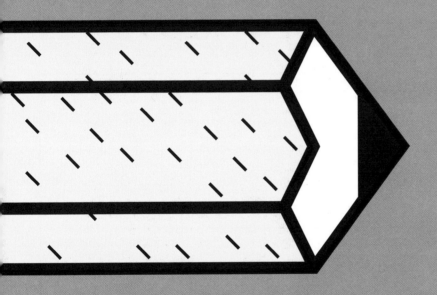

PUZZLES

1997, Japan

New Zealander Wayne Gould falls in love with *Sudoku* after spotting it in a magazine in Tokyo.

2004, New Zealand

Wayne Gould develops a computer program that provides puzzles to the *London Times*, marking the official start to Sudoku Mania!

2011, United States

Nikoli introduces *Visual Sudoku*, the next evolution for the famous logic game.

ROCK AROUND THE CLOCK

1 2 3 4 5 6 7 8 9

Keeping Time
With hands 9- and 14-feet-long and each of its four dials 23 feet across, Big Ben's flawless timekeeping is regulated by a simple stack of coins on the clock's pendulum.

CARPE SUDOKUM

I	II	III	IV	V	VI	VII	VIII	IX
1	2	3	4	5	6	7	8	9

III	IV	*VII*	V	IX	II		I	
IX	*✓*	VI				III		II
I	VIII	*IV*					V	
II			I		III			VII
V				VI				IV
VIII			II		VII			I
VII	I						VI	
IV		V				I		III
VI	III		IV	VII	I		II	

ALL HAIL BRAILLE

GETTING OLD SCHOOLED

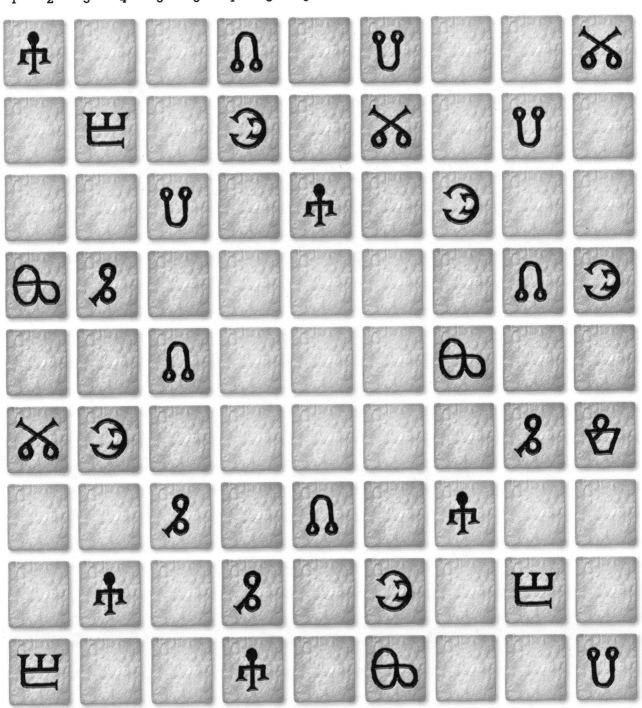

THE DOMINO EFFECT

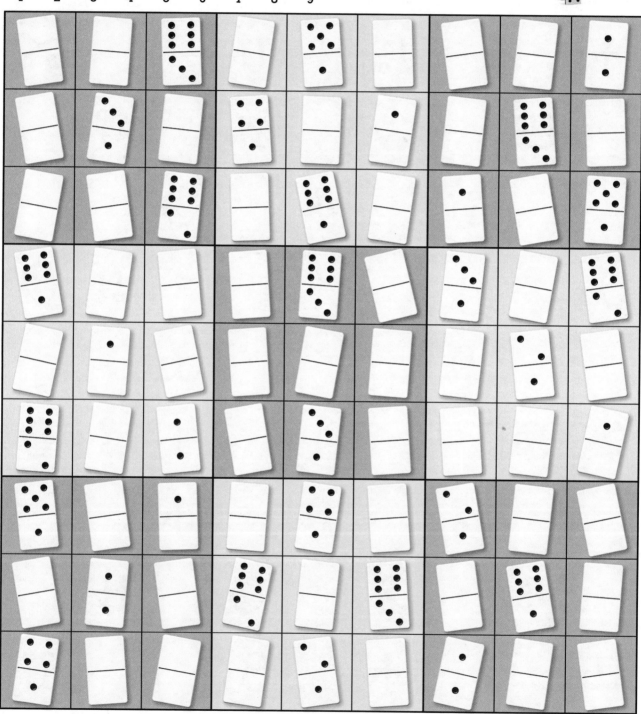

For the Win!
On August 18, 2003, Ma Li Hua set the Guinness World Record for the longest domino chain toppled by a single person. Of the total 303,628 tiles, just seven were left standing!

WHAT'S YOUR SIGN?

Signs Worth a Thousand Words
Koko, the famous 300-pound gorilla, has an American Sign Language (ASL) vocabulary of more than 1,000 words. She can gesture for food, water, and even that she has a cavity!

JUST MY TYPE

! @ # $ % ∧ & ✲ (
1   2   3   4   5   6   7   8   9

The Key to History
Though Christopher Latham Sholes is often credited with the invention of the typewriter, at least 52 other designs had been created before his model.

		(	&		%	!		
		%	!		#	✲		
∧	!						#	%
%	&		✲				$	!
			%		&			
!	@			(			%	∧
(	#						!	&
		!	@		(	∧		
		@	$		!	%		

THE ELEMENTS OF STYLE

1.0079 H HYDROGEN	4.0026 He HELIUM	6.941 Li LITHIUM	9.0122 Be BERYLLIUM	10.811 B BORON	12.011 C CARBON	14.007 N NITROGEN	15.999 O OXYGEN	18.998 F FLUORINE
1	2	3	4	5	6	7	8	9

At the Head of the Table
Carbon, atomic number 6 on the Periodic Table, has such unique bonding properties that it can form more organic chemical compounds than any other element.

1	2	3	4	5	6	7	8	9
					1.0079 H HYDROGEN		9.0122 Be BERYLLIUM	6.941 Li LITHIUM
12.011 C CARBON	4.0026 He HELIUM		10.811 B BORON				15.999 O OXYGEN	
6.941 Li LITHIUM		10.811 B BORON	18.998 F FLUORINE			4.0026 He HELIUM		
						10.811 B BORON	1.0079 H HYDROGEN	
14.007 N NITROGEN								12.011 C CARBON
	15.999 O OXYGEN	4.0026 He HELIUM						
		9.0122 Be BERYLLIUM			6.941 Li LITHIUM	18.998 F FLUORINE		15.999 O OXYGEN
	1.0079 H HYDROGEN				14.007 N NITROGEN		4.0026 He HELIUM	9.0122 Be BERYLLIUM
	12.011 C CARBON	15.999 O OXYGEN	10.811 B BORON					

SWING FOR THE FENCE!

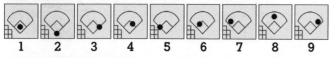

For the Fans
In the early 1860s, Union soldiers fighting in the Civil War helped spread baseball's popularity to different parts of the country, playing during their time off.

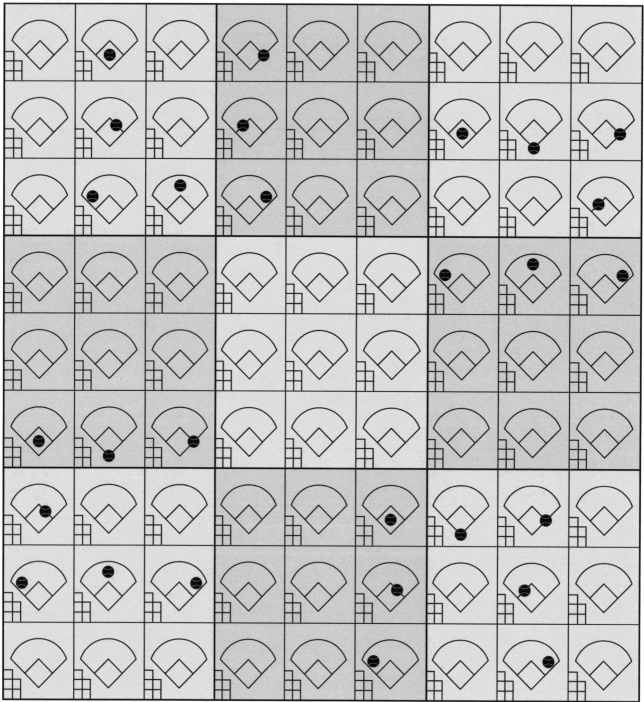

#*	ABC	DEF	GHI	JKL	MNO	PQRS	TUV	WXYZ
1	2	3	4	5	6	7	8	9

Such Phonies
Today, it's not uncommon for each person in the U.S. to have multiple telephones (work, home, cell), but dial back to 1914, and there were fewer than 10 phones per 100 people.

		PQRS			GHI		#*	
		TUV		JKL			DEF	GHI
#*	JKL					ABC		
					ABC			MNO
	PQRS			DEF			GHI	
DEF			#*					
		JKL					ABC	DEF
MNO	TUV			GHI		JKL		
	ABC		PQRS			#*		

PLAYING WITH A FULL DECK

House of Cards
The tallest freestanding playing-card house, built by Bryan Berg on October 14, 2007, reached more than 25 feet tall.

CAST OF CHARACTERS

一 二 三 四 五 六 七 八 九
1　2　3　4　5　6　7　8　9

Different Strokes
Some Japanese calligraphers use locks from a baby's first haircut as bristles in a brush, or *fude*.

五	一						四	三
			九	七		八	六	
				一				
			三		六		四	
七			三		四			二
			二		九		一	
					七			
			四	一		三	二	
二	六						五	一

ROCK AROUND THE CLOCK

1 2 3 4 5 6 7 8 9

Too Much Time on Their Hands

The system we now know as Standard Time was created in 1884, when members of 27 countries met in Washington, D.C., to solve problems caused by the varying standards.

CARPE SUDOKUM

Mysterious Beginnings
The origin of Roman numerals is obscure, but according to 19th century German historian Theodor Mommsen, they are derived in part from the Greek and Latin alphabet.

I	II	III	IV	V	VI	VII	VIII	IX
1	2	3	4	5	6	7	8	9

I					V			II
	VII						IV	
				II	VI			
VII				III		I	VI	
			II		IX		VIII	
			I	IV		II		III
					V	VII		
	VI						I	
III					I			V

ALL HAIL BRAILLE

1 2 3 4 5 6 7 8 9

A Posthumous Honor
The Braille code wouldn't be recognized as the official method of reading and writing for the blind until 1854, two years after the death of Louis Braille.

GETTING OLD SCHOOLED

Etched in Stone
The Baška Tablet, housed at the Croatian Academy of Sciences and Arts in Zagreb, dates from about 1100, and is the oldest (and longest) known example of Glagolitic script in the world.

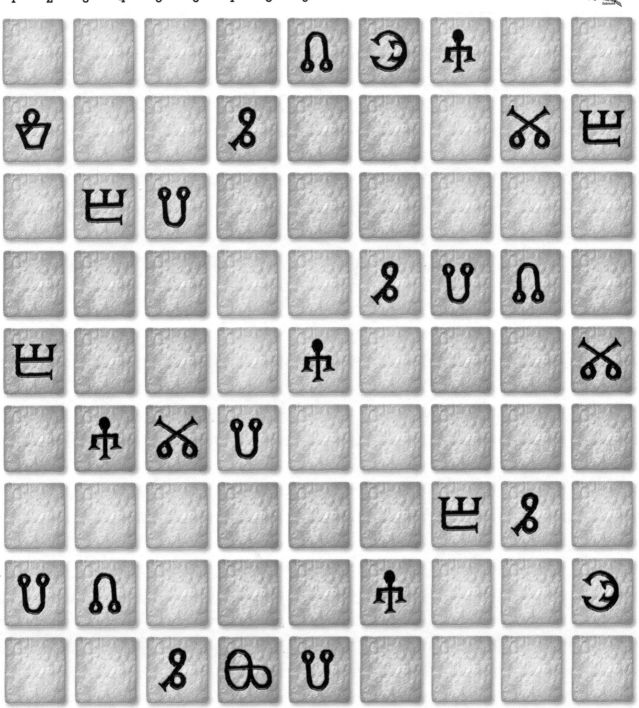

THE DOMINO EFFECT

Ancient Games
Though its origins are unclear, the game of dominoes likely dates back to 12th century China; the game as we know it now became popular in Europe in the 18th century.

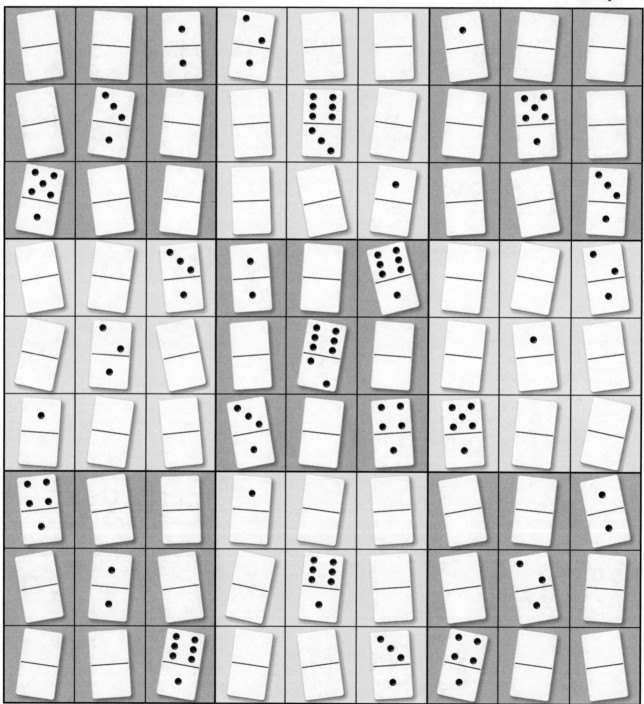

WHAT'S YOUR SIGN?

I Sign Tomato, You Sign Tomato, Too!
Because their signs represent concepts and not words, sign languages from different countries have more in common with other sign languages than with their corresponding spoken languages.

JUST MY TYPE

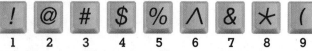

!	@	#	$	%	∧	&	*	(
1	2	3	4	5	6	7	8	9

Bang, Pow to Click, Clack
In April 1874, American gun manufacturer E. Remington & Sons shipped its first model "Type Writer," based on a prototype by American inventor Christopher Latham Sholes.

!				&				∧
		$				@		
	&		#		(		*	
#			&		*			@
		*		$		%		
$			@		!			*
	!		*			$		#
		#					!	
@				!				&

THE ELEMENTS OF STYLE

Whether 'Tis Nobler
British chemist Sir William Ramsay is credited for isolating all of the noble gases (the most stable of the elements) except radon.

| 1.0079 H HYDROGEN — 1 | 4.0026 He HELIUM — 2 | 6.941 Li LITHIUM — 3 | 9.0122 Be BERYLLIUM — 4 | 10.811 B BORON — 5 | 12.011 C CARBON — 6 | 14.007 N NITROGEN — 7 | 15.999 O OXYGEN — 8 | 18.998 F FLUORINE — 9 |

				10.811 B BORON	4.0026 He HELIUM		1.0079 H HYDROGEN	
	10.811 B BORON	4.0026 He HELIUM			9.0122 Be BERYLLIUM		12.011 C CARBON	
14.007 N NITROGEN				6.941 Li LITHIUM			18.998 F FLUORINE	
	18.998 F FLUORINE		15.999 O OXYGEN		1.0079 H HYDROGEN			14.007 N NITROGEN
10.811 B BORON		1.0079 H HYDROGEN				18.998 F FLUORINE		12.011 C CARBON
9.0122 Be BERYLLIUM			4.0026 He HELIUM		10.811 B BORON		15.999 O OXYGEN	
	6.941 Li LITHIUM			9.0122 Be BERYLLIUM				18.998 F FLUORINE
	1.0079 H HYDROGEN		12.011 C CARBON			4.0026 He HELIUM	6.941 Li LITHIUM	
		9.0122 Be BERYLLIUM		1.0079 H HYDROGEN	15.999 O OXYGEN			

SWING FOR THE FENCE!

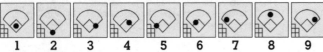

1 2 3 4 5 6 7 8 9

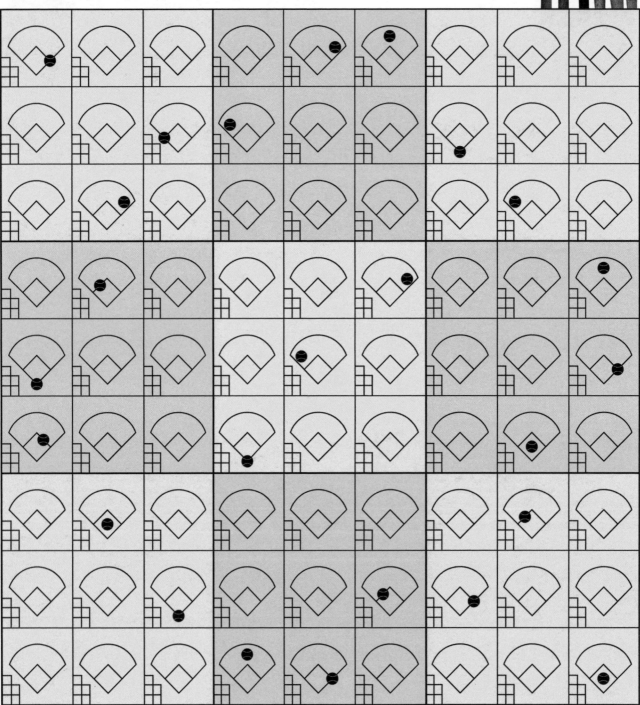

SPEED DIAL

#*	ABC	DEF	GHI	JKL	MNO	PQRS	TUV	WXYZ
1	2	3	4	5	6	7	8	9

Race to the Finish
Alexander Graham Bell and Elisha Gray rushed to patent their discoveries—both devices an "improvement in telegraphy"—within hours of each other. Bell won the ensuing legal battle.

ABC			DEF			#*		
	#*			JKL	WXYZ			
	DEF						PQRS	
#*			MNO			DEF		JKL
				GHI				
DEF		TUV			PQRS			GHI
	MNO						ABC	
			GHI	ABC			#*	
		GHI			#*			DEF

PLAYING WITH A FULL DECK

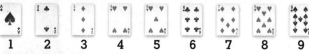

1 2 3 4 5 6 7 8 9

This Deck's on Fire
Card-playing was an illegal activity in 15th century Europe; in fact, in 1423, St. Bernardino of Sienna held a public card-burning event in Bologna, Italy.

CAST OF CHARACTERS

一 二 三 四 五 六 七 八 九
1　2　3　4　5　6　7　8　9

The Sudoku Nine
Fall seven times, stand up eight.
—Japanese Proverb

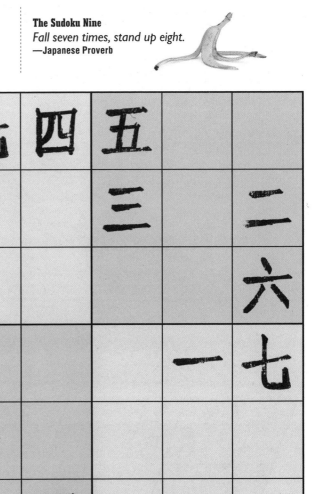

SUDO-KUBE

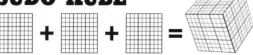 + + =

It's Hip to Be Cube
Cubism is a 20th-century art movement in which artists represented a 3-D universe on a flat canvas, defying previous conventions of form and space.

ROCK AROUND THE CLOCK

1 2 3 4 5 6 7 8 9

Vintage Flair
The first portable timepieces appeared around 1500 and were made mostly in Germany and France; they often had only one hand and were worn on a chain around the neck.

CARPE SUDOKUM

I	II	III	IV	V	VI	VII	VIII	IX
1	2	3	4	5	6	7	8	9

	II			I			VI	
VIII			VII		IX			IV
		IV				II		
	IV		V		I		VII	
II				VI				IX
	IX		II		VII		V	
		V				I		
IX			III		II			V
	VI			VIII			IV	

ALL HAIL BRAILLE

Precious Instruments
Louis Braille's hands are entombed in Coupvray, separately from the rest of his body, which is interred at the Panthéon in Paris.

1 2 3 4 5 6 7 8 9

EASY 29

GETTING OLD SCHOOLED

Know Your ABCs
The word "glagolitic" derives from the Croatian name for alphabet, *glagoljica.* It's commonly believed that Saints Cyril and Methodius invented and named the Glagolitic alphabet.

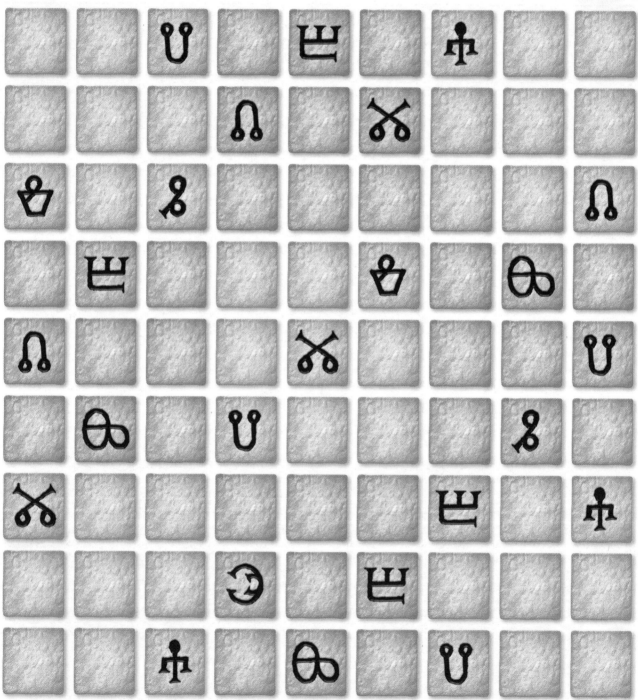

THE DOMINO EFFECT

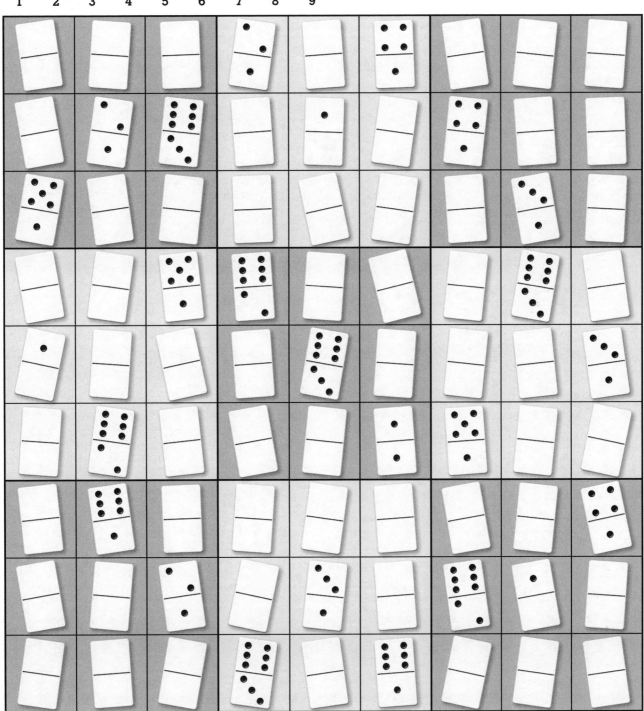

WHAT'S YOUR SIGN?

1 2 3 4 5 6 7 8 9

Hand Signal, then Hut

Football quarterback Peyton Manning is known for his use of hand signals, which serve as clear instructions to his teammates during games at particularly noisy stadiums.

JUST MY TYPE

!	@	#	$	%	∧	&	*	(
1	2	3	4	5	6	7	8	9

Typewritten Manuscripts, Lost and Found
Gone With the Wind author Margaret Mitchell instructed her husband to burn the book's original manuscript, but the last four chapters survived, discovered 75 years after the novel's publication.

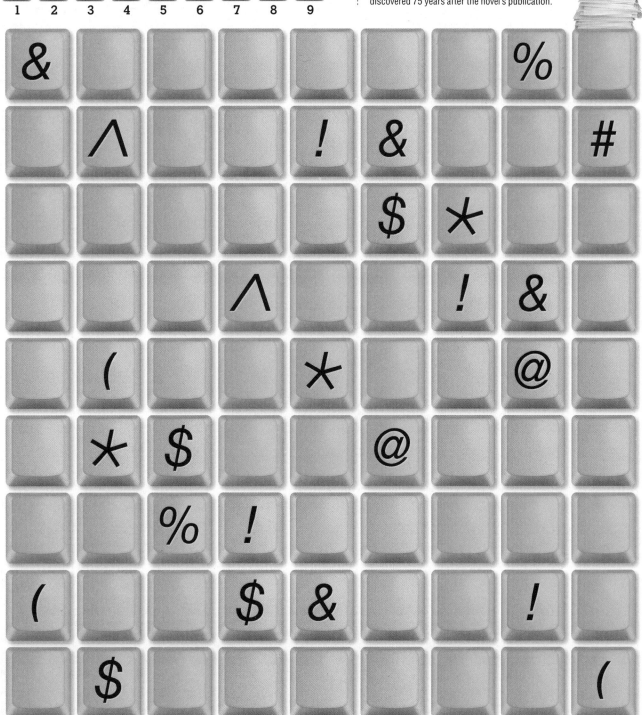

THE ELEMENTS OF STYLE

1.0079 H HYDROGEN	4.0026 He HELIUM	6.941 Li LITHIUM	9.0122 Be BERYLLIUM	10.811 B BORON	12.011 C CARBON	14.007 N NITROGEN	15.999 O OXYGEN	18.998 F FLUORINE
1	2	3	4	5	6	7	8	9

A Work in Progress
In 1869, Dmitri Mendeleev published the first Periodic Table of Elements, containing 65 elements. Today's Periodic Table has 118, and new elements are still being discovered.

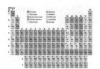

		He				Be	F	
	B			He			C	
Li			C					N
		N						H
	C			Li		B		
F					Li			
N				Li				B
	O		N			Be		
		B	Be			C		

SWING FOR THE FENCE!

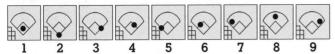

1   2   3   4   5   6   7   8   9

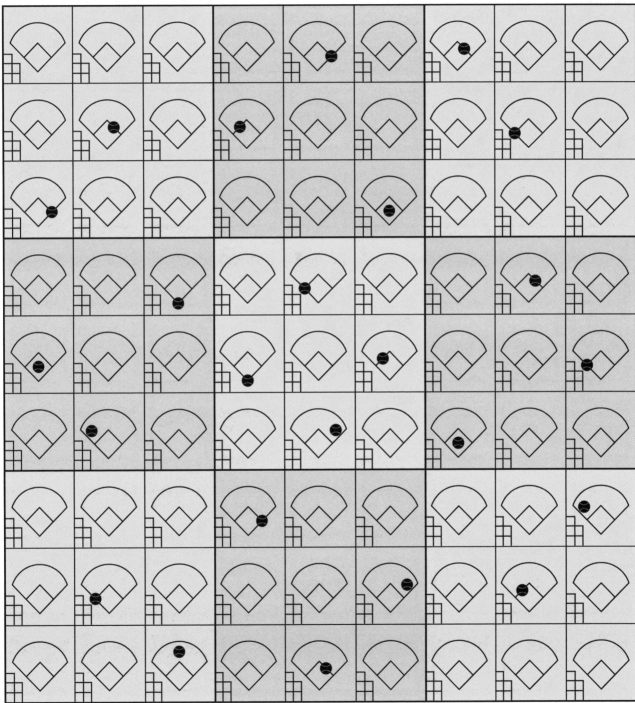

SPEED DIAL

Elementary, My Dear Watson
On March 10, 1876, Alexander Graham Bell called Thomas A. Watson, who was in the next room. "Mr. Watson, come here. I want to see you," were the first words conveyed via telephone.

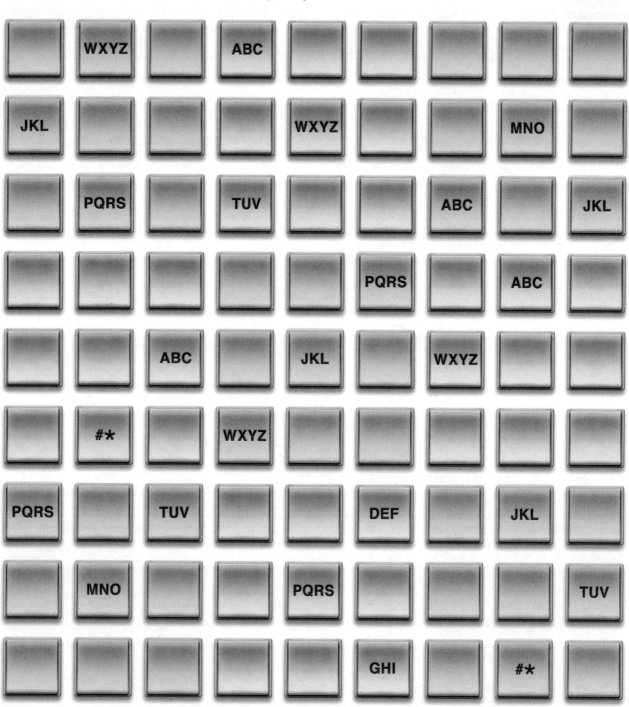

PLAYING WITH A FULL DECK

1   2   3   4   5   6   7   8   9

Eyes on the Prize
Dominic O'Brien set a world record on November 26, 1993, when he memorized 40 decks of cards in a single sighting. He made only one mistake.

一	二	三	四	五	六	七	八	九
1	2	3	4	5	6	7	8	9

The Way of Tea
Calligraphic scrolls are hung in the alcove of a tearoom to welcome guests to a Japanese Tea Ceremony. The writing on the scrolls is meant to reflect upon or illuminate the ceremony.

		六				五	二	
	八			七			六	
一			八					三
八						六		
	五			一		七		
		三						九
三					七			二
	二			六			一	
		五	一			四		

ROCK AROUND THE CLOCK

1   2   3   4   5   6   7   8   9

All the Time in the World
Studies show that when long-term smokers quit, their perception of time expands by half, due to an underlying link between biological and psychological processes.

CARPE SUDOKUM

I	II	III	IV	V	VI	VII	VIII	IX
1	2	3	4	5	6	7	8	9

		II			V			VI
	IX			VIII		III		
III							V	
	V				VI			II
		IX		I		VI		
II			VII				VIII	
	VIII							III
		III		IX			VII	
VI			III			I		

ALL HAIL BRAILLE

1 2 3 4 5 6 7 8 9

Dot to Dot
Braille characters are based on a rectangular arrangement of six dot positions in two columns of three dots each; dots can be raised to create 64 possible combinations.

GETTING OLD SCHOOLED

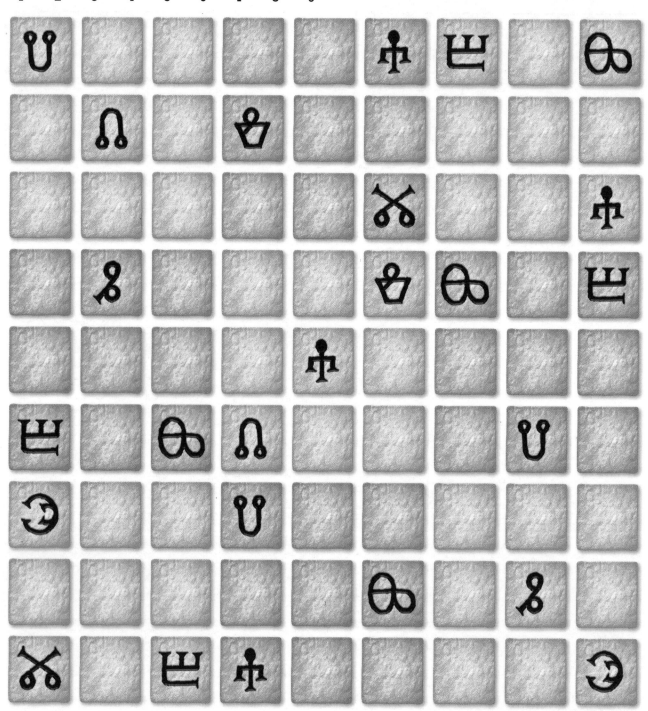

THE DOMINO EFFECT

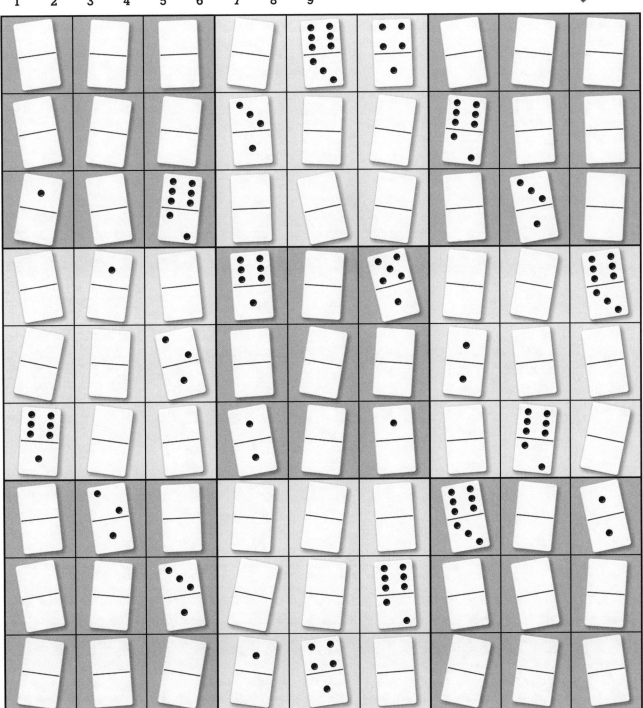

The Fall Heard 'Round the World
4,491,863 dominoes fell to set a world record on Domino Day 2009. The dominoes took one and a half hours to fall, and performed all kinds of unusual feats, including climbing stairs.

EASY 🏠 43

WHAT'S YOUR SIGN?

1 2 3 4 5 6 7 8 9

Parlez-vous Français?
Despite the fact that the U.S. and Britain share a spoken language, American Sign Language has more signs and gestures in common with French Sign Language.

JUST MY TYPE

!	@	#	$	%	∧	&	✳	(
1	2	3	4	5	6	7	8	9

Sometimes the Best Inventions Are Accidents
Many early typewriter designs were created to make reading possible for the blind, not to mechanize handwriting.

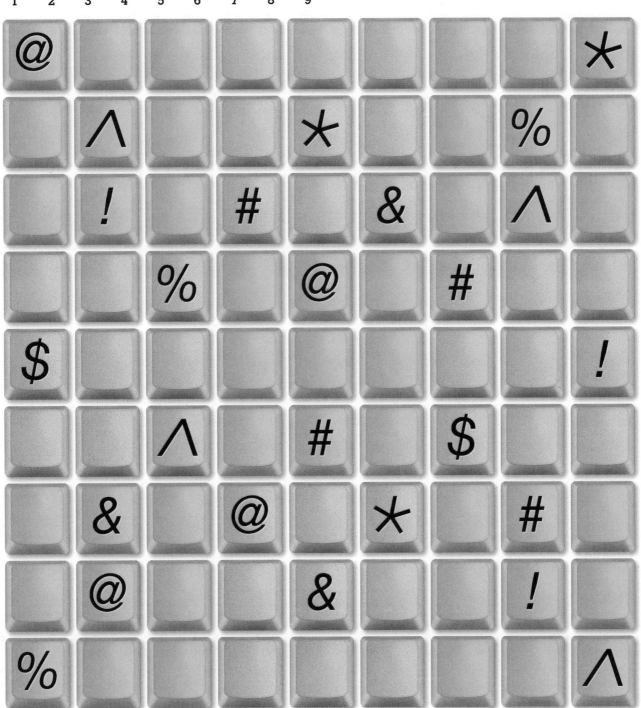

THE ELEMENTS OF STYLE

1.0079 H HYDROGEN	4.0026 He HELIUM	6.941 Li LITHIUM	9.0122 Be BERYLLIUM	10.811 B BORON	12.011 C CARBON	14.007 N NITROGEN	15.999 O OXYGEN	18.998 F FLUORINE
1	2	3	4	5	6	7	8	9

Back to the Basics
Hydrogen was the first element and remains the most common in the universe today. Hydrogen and helium create all other elements inside the nuclei of stars via nuclear fusion reactions.

	6.941 Li LITHIUM			9.0122 Be BERYLLIUM			18.998 F FLUORINE	
10.811 B BORON								14.007 N NITROGEN
		18.998 F FLUORINE		14.007 N NITROGEN		1.0079 H HYDROGEN		
	14.007 N NITROGEN		10.811 B BORON		18.998 F FLUORINE	4.0026 He HELIUM		
9.0122 Be BERYLLIUM				15.999 O OXYGEN				18.998 F FLUORINE
	12.011 C CARBON		1.0079 H HYDROGEN		9.0122 Be BERYLLIUM		10.811 B BORON	
		15.999 O OXYGEN		12.011 C CARBON		9.0122 Be BERYLLIUM		
12.011 C CARBON								10.811 B BORON
	9.0122 Be BERYLLIUM			10.811 B BORON			15.999 O OXYGEN	

SWING FOR THE FENCE!

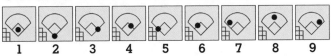

1 2 3 4 5 6 7 8 9

Baseball's Beginnings
The Boston Pilgrims took on the Pittsburgh Pirates in the first modern World Series at Huntington Avenue Base Ball Grounds in Boston in 1903.

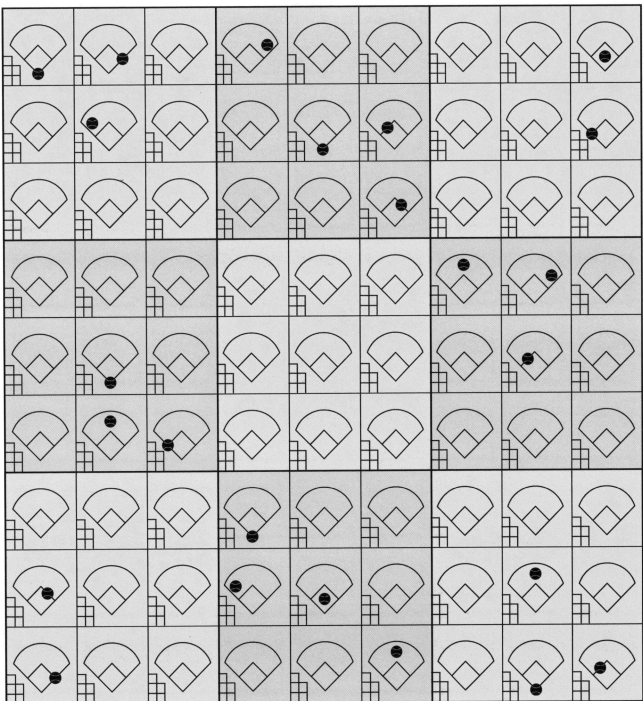

SPEED DIAL

#*	ABC	DEF	GHI	JKL	MNO	PQRS	TUV	WXYZ
1	2	3	4	5	6	7	8	9

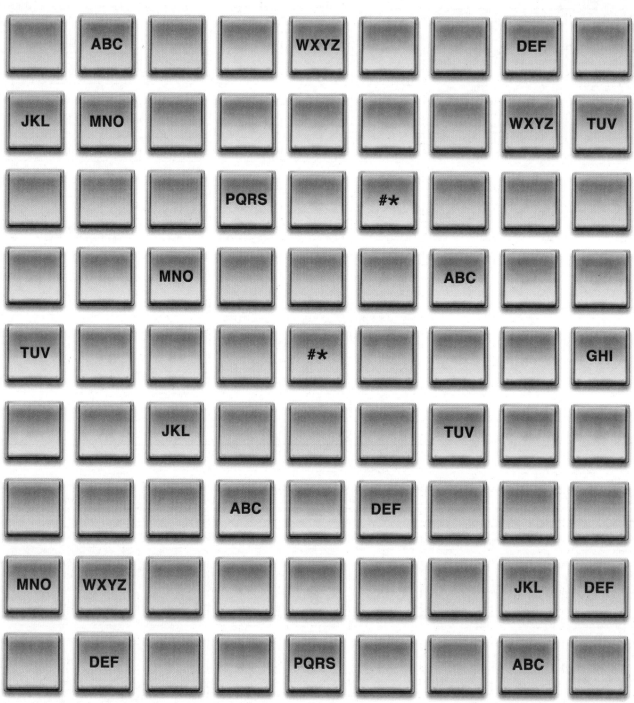

PLAYING WITH A FULL DECK

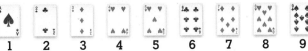

| 1 | 2 | 3 | 4 | 5 | 6 | 7 | 8 | 9 |

Temperature's Rising
Ralf Laue held the largest card fan in the world on March 18, 1994, when he fanned 326 cards in one hand—a move that made every card he was holding visible.

CAST OF CHARACTERS

一	二	三	四	五	六	七	八	九
1	2	3	4	5	6	7	8	9

Good Golly, a Dolly!
1,300 years after Japanese Emperor Kotoku's visit to Arima Springs and the subsequent birth of his son, Arima locals continue to make specialty brushes with a doll that springs from the handle.

		三				四		
	五			六			一	
四			二					九
		二			三		八	
	八			四			三	
七			九			五		
三					六			五
	四			五			七	
		七				二		

Recipe for Failure
There are more than 43 quintillion possible *wrong* answers to a Rubik's Cube.

ROCK AROUND THE CLOCK

1 2 3 4 5 6 7 8 9

CARPE SUDOKUM

I	II	III	IV	V	VI	VII	VIII	IX
1	2	3	4	5	6	7	8	9

Toga Party!
The Romans were highly influenced by the Etruscans, and adopted from them not only an early form of Roman numerals, but the art of gladiatorial combat and the toga.

	III	V						
		VI			IX			V
				VII	IV		II	III
II	III							
	IX		V			II		
						IX	IV	
VII	IX		IV	II				
VI			I			IV		
							VIII	VI

ALL HAIL BRAILLE

Eyes Worldwide
Of the 284 million people in the world who fall on the spectrum of severe visual impairment, 39 million are completely blind.

GETTING OLD SCHOOLED

Glagolitic Is Slav for Special
In 1248, Pope Innocent IV gave Croatians special permission to use their own language in liturgy; other vernacular languages couldn't be used in religious ceremonies until the 1960s.

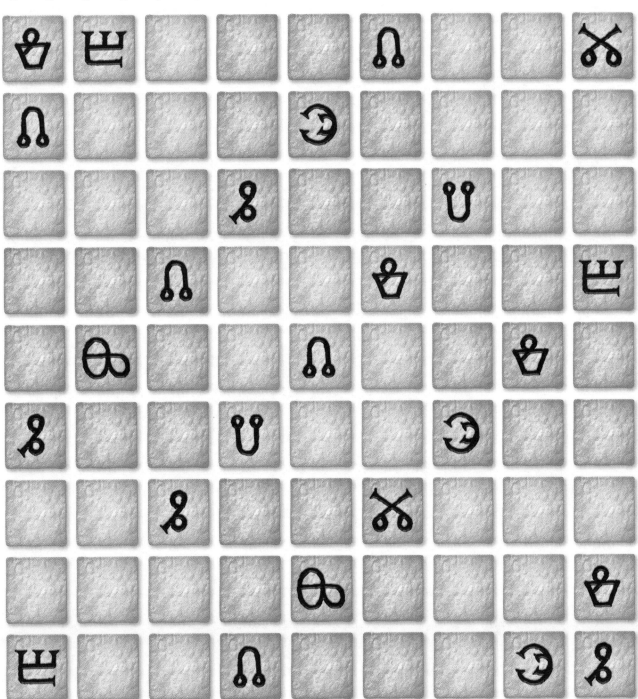

THE DOMINO EFFECT

Lean on Me
The longest human domino line was formed by an impressive 10,267 participants at the Ordos International Nadam Fair in Ordos City, China, on August 12, 2010.

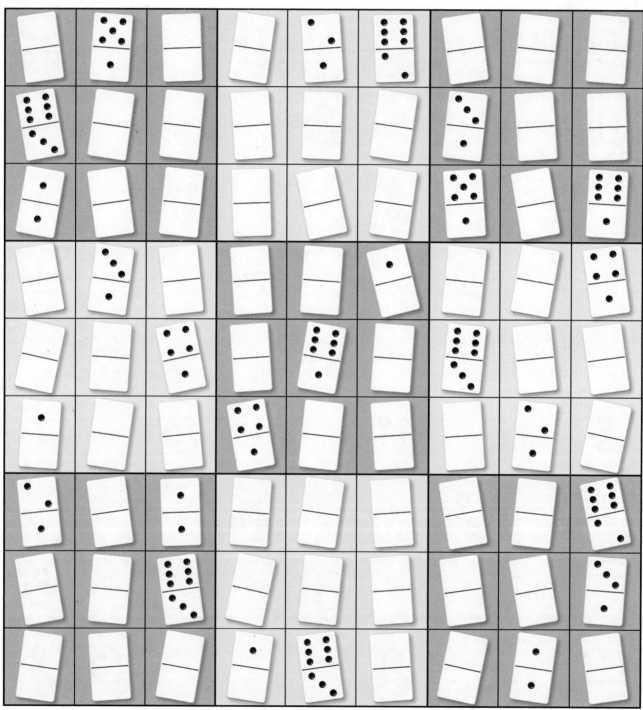

WHAT'S YOUR SIGN?

1   2   3   4   5   6   7   8   9

I'd Like to Thank the Academy
At 21, Marlee Matlin became the youngest recipient of the Best Actress Oscar when she won the statue for her role in *Children of a Lesser God* (1986). She signed her acceptance speech.

	3		7					
		4		2				7
			4		5		1	
		7				1		4
	4			3			2	
3		2				5		
	2		1		7			
4				5		4		
					2		4	

EASY   57

JUST MY TYPE

!	@	#	$	%	∧	&	*	(
1	2	3	4	5	6	7	8	9

A Rose by Any Other Name
Early typewriter inventions had many various names—like machine kryptographique and universal compositor—before the word "typewriter" became universal.

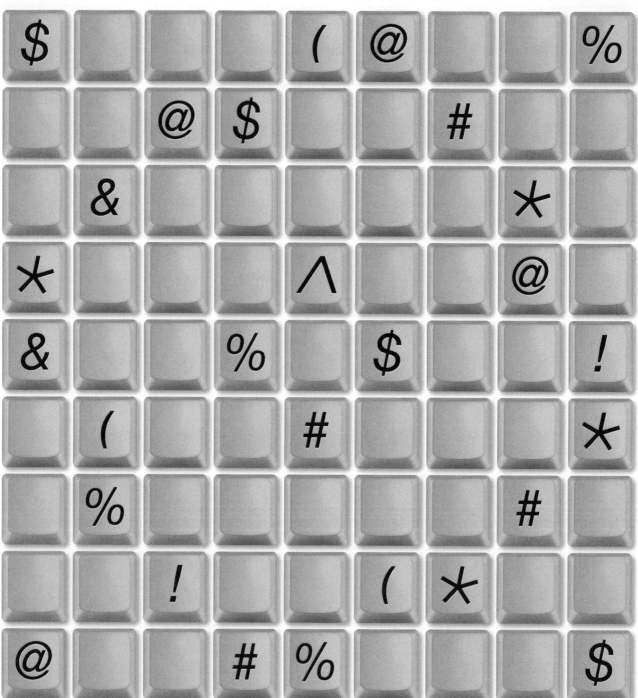

THE ELEMENTS OF STYLE

1.0079	4.0026	6.941	9.0122	10.811	12.011	14.007	15.999	18.998
H	He	Li	Be	B	C	N	O	F
HYDROGEN	HELIUM	LITHIUM	BERYLLIUM	BORON	CARBON	NITROGEN	OXYGEN	FLUORINE
1	2	3	4	5	6	7	8	9

Carbon Is a Girl's Best Friend
Carbon occurs in all living organisms and is formed in the interiors of stars. After many years at very high pressure it becomes something nearly as sparkly: a diamond.

	B (10.811) BORON				Li (6.941) LITHIUM			F (18.998) FLUORINE
		C (12.011) CARBON		H (1.0079) HYDROGEN				
Li (6.941) LITHIUM			He (4.0026) HELIUM			C (12.011) CARBON		
		Li (6.941) LITHIUM			B (10.811) BORON			He (4.0026) HELIUM
	O (15.999) OXYGEN			He (4.0026) HELIUM			Li (6.941) LITHIUM	
He (4.0026) HELIUM			Be (9.0122) BERYLLIUM			H (1.0079) HYDROGEN		
		H (1.0079) HYDROGEN			N (14.007) NITROGEN			Be (9.0122) BERYLLIUM
				O (15.999) OXYGEN		B (10.811) BORON		
Be (9.0122) BERYLLIUM			B (10.811) BORON				H (1.0079) HYDROGEN	

SWING FOR THE FENCE!

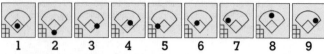

1 2 3 4 5 6 7 8 9

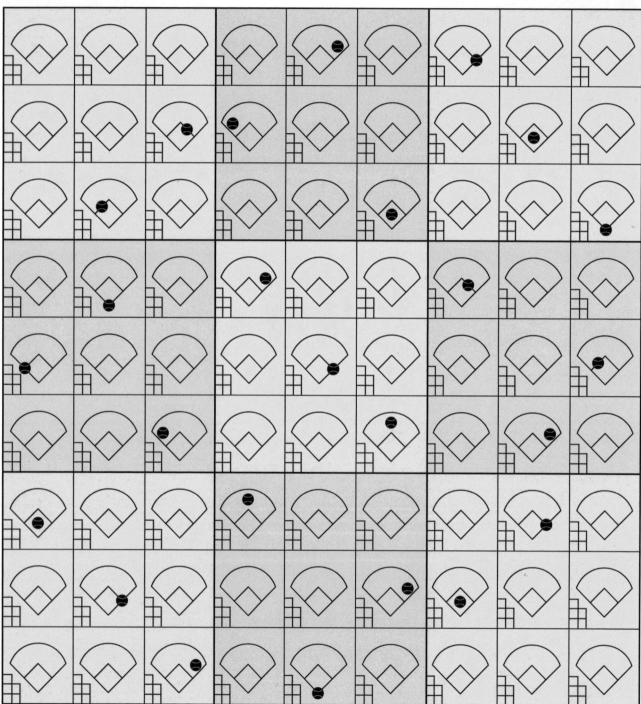

SPEED DIAL

#*	ABC	DEF	GHI	JKL	MNO	PQRS	TUV	WXYZ
1	2	3	4	5	6	7	8	9

Identity Crisis
The millions of people who screen calls can thank Carolyn Doughty of Bell Labs. In 1982, she patented Caller ID in the United States.

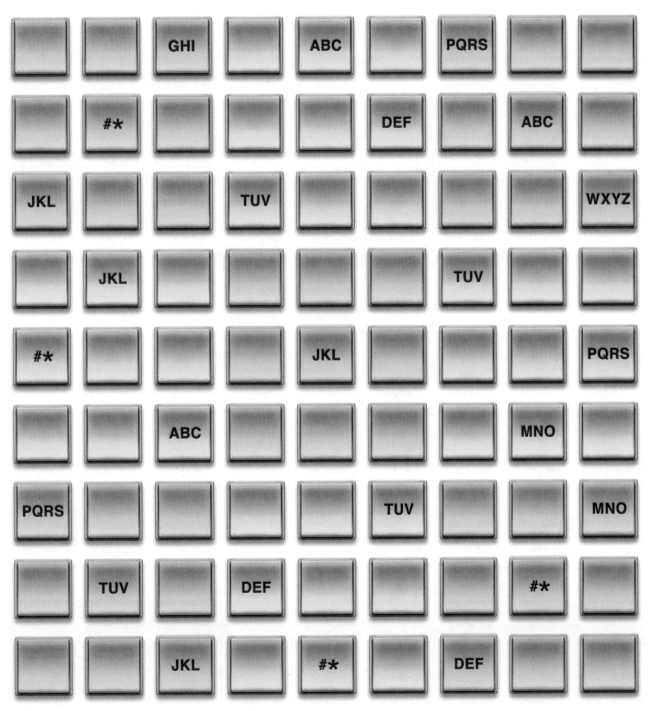

PLAYING WITH A FULL DECK

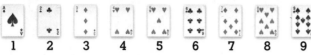

1 2 3 4 5 6 7 8 9

That's No Gamble
The most expensive deck of cards, believed to be the oldest complete deck in existence, was sold for $143,352 to New York's Metropolitan Museum of Art at a 1983 auction in Sotheby's London.

CAST OF CHARACTERS

一	二	三	四	五	六	七	八	九
1	2	3	4	5	6	7	8	9

Peace via Origami
Sadako and the Thousand Paper Cranes is based on the true story of Sadako Sasaki, who attempted to fold 1,000 paper cranes in order to be granted a wish for recovery from her illness.

	六	九					三	
二			六	八				九
一					四			
	三					四		
	七			四			五	
		六					七	
			三					二
四				一	六			七
	一					五	九	

ROCK AROUND THE CLOCK

1   2   3   4   5   6   7   8   9

An Heirloom Piece

The grandfather clock, or long case clock, derives its name from a popular 1876 song "My Grandfather's Clock," written by Henry Clay Work and later covered by Johnny Cash.

CARPE SUDOKUM

	I	II	III	IV	V	VI	VII	VIII	IX
	1	2	3	4	5	6	7	8	9
		VII			IV		II		
		VI				II		V	VII
	I					VII			
		VIII	I						
	V				VII				II
							VIII	I	
				III					IX
	III	V		I				VI	
			IV		V			VIII	

ALL HAIL BRAILLE

1   2   3   4   5   6   7   8   9

Hardship Leads to Innovation

Louis Braille became blind at the age of three when he poked himself in the eye with a sharp awl. He lost sight in both eyes when an infection from the injury spread.

GETTING OLD SCHOOLED

A Stepping Stone
The Glagolitic alphabet is thought to be the oldest Slavic alphabet. It is the predecessor to the Cyrillic alphabet, which is still used in most Slavic languages.

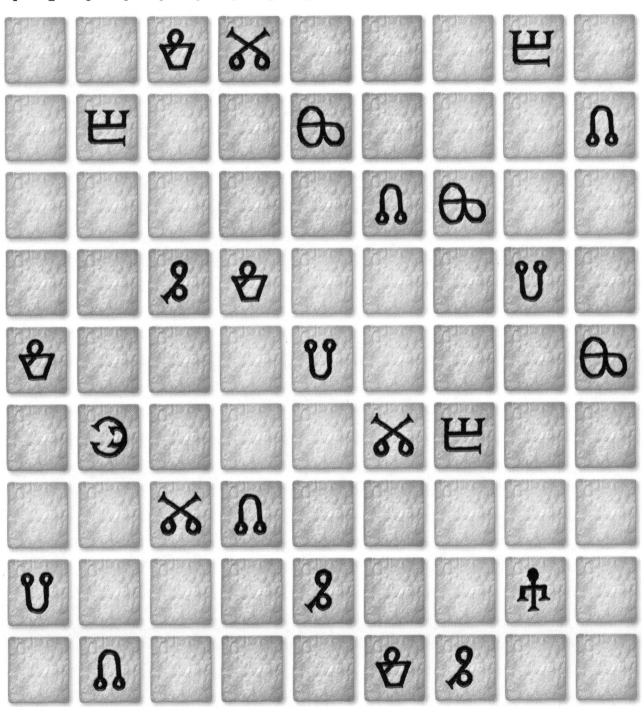

THE DOMINO EFFECT

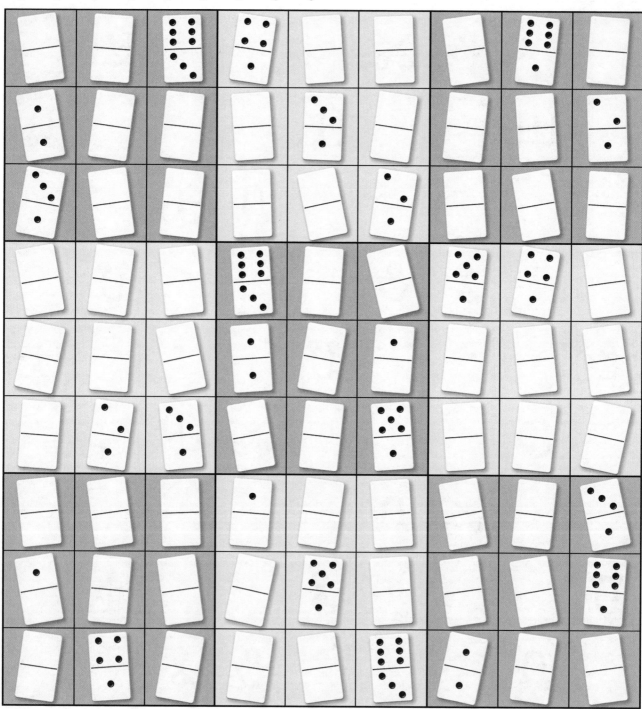

WHAT'S YOUR SIGN?

1 2 3 4 5 6 7 8 9

Lefty, Righty
Like spoken language, sign language is controlled primarily by the left side of the brain—despite the fact that it is a more visual, traditionally right-brain neurological exercise.

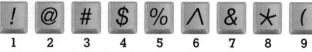
Old Keys Die Hard
The QWERTY keyboard exists today because it had no competition from 1874 to 1881. By the time other models were created, typists weren't interested in learning a new system.

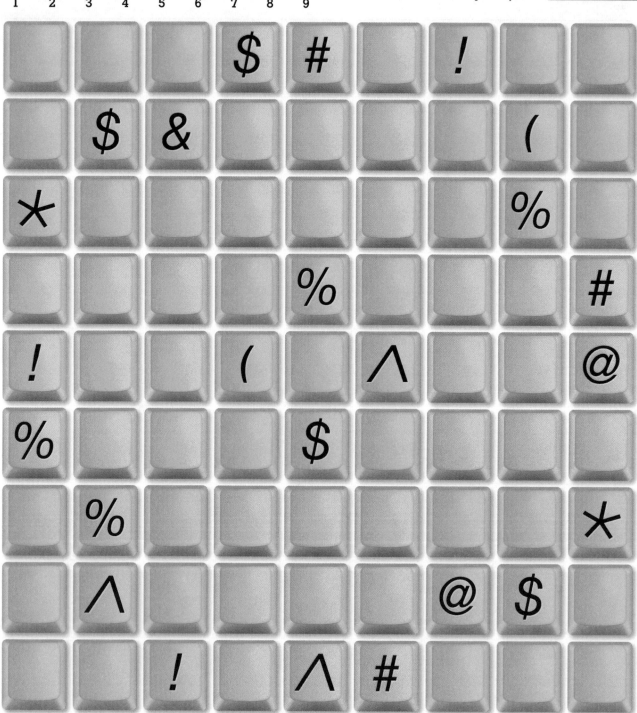

THE ELEMENTS OF STYLE

1.0079	4.0026	6.941	9.0122	10.811	12.011	14.007	15.999	18.998
H	He	Li	Be	B	C	N	O	F
HYDROGEN	HELIUM	LITHIUM	BERYLLIUM	BORON	CARBON	NITROGEN	OXYGEN	FLUORINE
1	**2**	**3**	**4**	**5**	**6**	**7**	**8**	**9**

Fang-tastic
Tellurium, an element first discovered in Transylvania, is known for its vampiric qualities. Half a microgram of tellurium in the air gives garlic breath to anyone inhaling it.

		12.011 C CARBON						6.941 Li LITHIUM
15.999 O OXYGEN	4.0026 He HELIUM			10.811 B BORON				
		9.0122 Be BERYLLIUM	15.999 O OXYGEN		12.011 C CARBON	10.811 B BORON		
	6.941 Li LITHIUM			18.998 F FLUORINE				
18.998 F FLUORINE		12.011 C CARBON			1.0079 H HYDROGEN			
	1.0079 H HYDROGEN			15.999 O OXYGEN				
6.941 Li LITHIUM	18.998 F FLUORINE		1.0079 H HYDROGEN	4.0026 He HELIUM				
		10.811 B BORON				14.007 N NITROGEN	18.998 F FLUORINE	
10.811 B BORON				4.0026 He HELIUM				

SWING FOR THE FENCE!

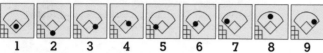

1 2 3 4 5 6 7 8 9

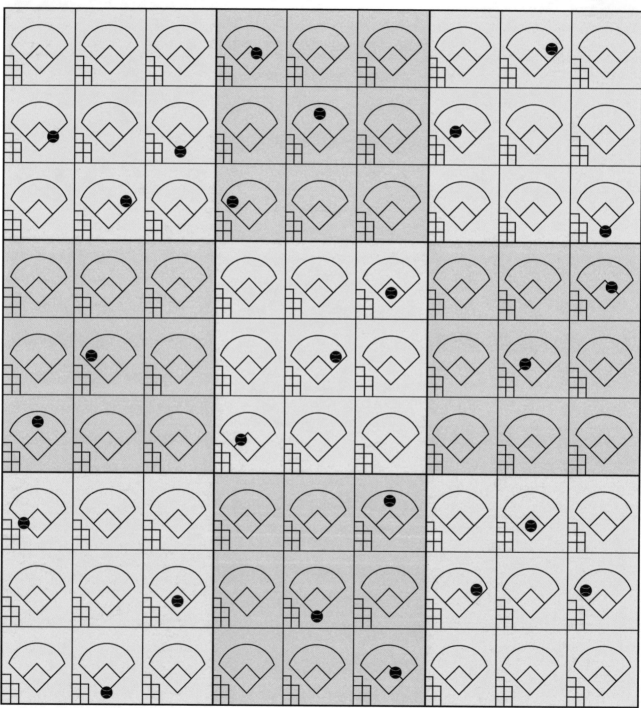

SPEED DIAL

#*	ABC	DEF	GHI	JKL	MNO	PQRS	TUV	WXYZ
1	2	3	4	5	6	7	8	9

Jenny, Are You There?
In 1982, the pop song "867-5309/Jenny" performed by Tommy Tutone hit #4 on the *Billboard* Hot 100—and caused a flurry of prank calls by folks looking for "Jenny" in every area code across the country.

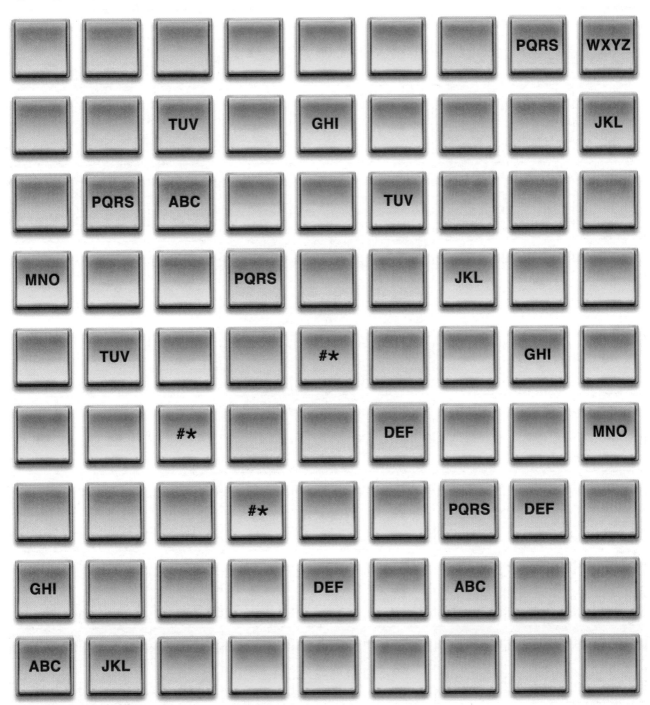

PLAYING WITH A FULL DECK

1   2   3   4   5   6   7   8   9

The Great Escape

During World War II, the U.S. Playing Card Company sent medical parcels to German POW camps containing decks of playing cards. Concealed maps with escape routes were hidden in the cards' layers.

CAST OF CHARACTERS

一	二	三	四	五	六	七	八	九
1	2	3	4	5	6	7	8	9

Star-Spangled Beginnings
Though popularized by the editors at Japanese game company Nikoli, Sudoku was originally adapted from a game called "Number Place" found in an American magazine.

	九	六					四	
			二	三				九
				七	三			
	四	一					七	三
			二					
二	七					五	八	
		二	五					
七					九	四		
	八					九	六	

SUDO-KUBE

ROCK AROUND THE CLOCK

1 2 3 4 5 6 7 8 9

CARPE SUDOKUM

What Does That Say?
In 1913, citing the difficulty many Americans had reading Roman numerals, the Secretary of the Treasury ordered the use of Arabic numerals on all public buildings.

Legend: I=1, II=2, III=3, IV=4, V=5, VI=6, VII=7, VIII=8, IX=9

I	II	III	IV	V	VI	VII	VIII	IX
1	2	3	4	5	6	7	8	9
	V	II					I	
			II	VI				III
					V	IV		
		VI	IX				VII	
III				IV				IX
	VII				I	II		
		IV	I					
VII				II	IV			
	II						V	VI

ALL HAIL BRAILLE

1 2 3 4 5 6 7 8 9

Feeling Punchy
Braille can be written by hand using a slate and stylus or punched by a Braille writer—a typewriter with only six keys and a space bar.

GETTING OLD SCHOOLED

ⴤ ⴖ ⴣ ⴕ ⴔ ⴤ ⴥ ⴜ ⴔ
1 2 3 4 5 6 7 8 9

Famous for Their Letters
The creators of the Glagolitic alphabet, Saints Cyril and Methodius, are often depicted with the scroll of an alphabet in icons that appear in many churches in eastern Europe.

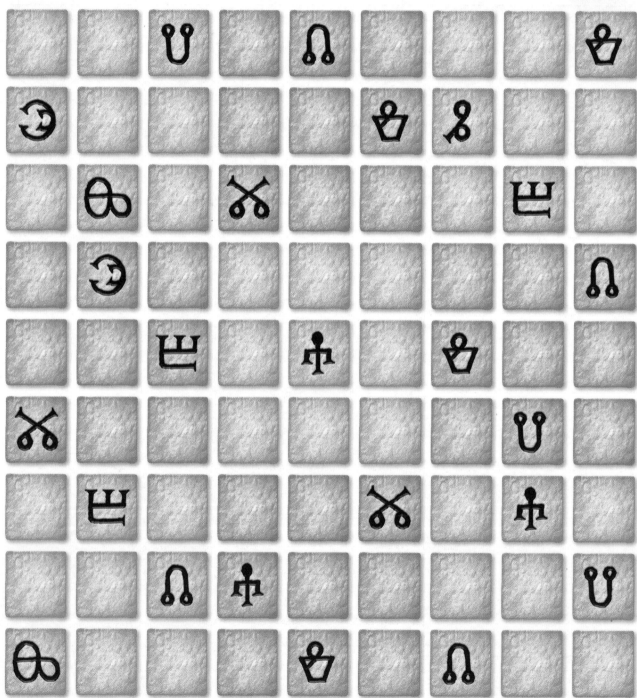

THE DOMINO EFFECT

Paris in the Springtime
*Of course I have played outdoor games.
I once played dominoes in an open air café
in Paris.* —Oscar Wilde

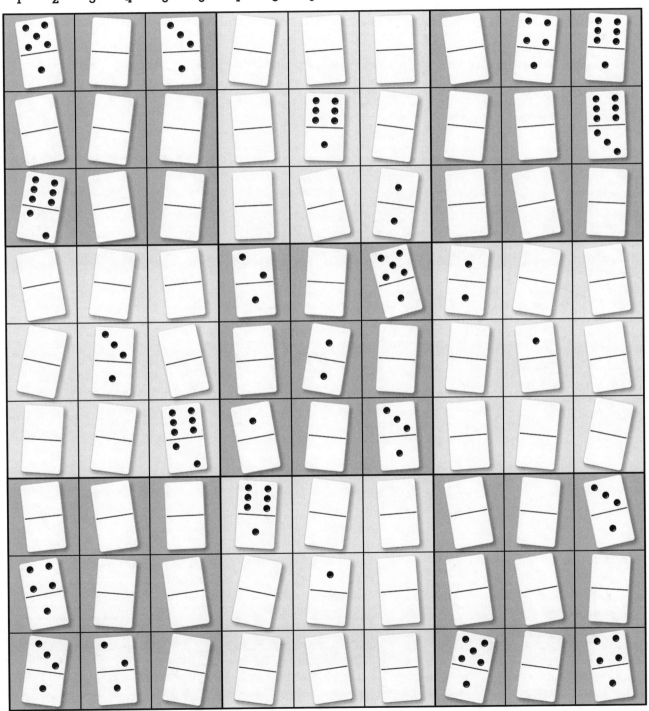

WHAT'S YOUR SIGN?

1 2 3 4 5 6 7 8 9

ASL on the Rise
According to the Modern Language Association (MLA), colleges have recently seen a 16 percent increase in the amount of hearing students studying American Sign Language.

JUST MY TYPE

!	@	#	$	%	∧	&	⋆	(
1	2	3	4	5	6	7	8	9

You've Got Mail!
In 1971 Ray Tomlinson used a system called Arpanet to send text from one computer to another over a network, a form of communication that would come to be known as e-mail.

E-mail

	%						@	
!			@			#		
		(				%		$
		&				(		⋆
	(			$			%	
#			%			@		
$		#				⋆		
		@				!		∧
	&							$

THE ELEMENTS OF STYLE

Banana Splitting Atom
Bananas are rich in potassium, which means they are very healthy. But, because a tiny percentage of potassium atoms are naturally radioactive, the fruit also can cause false alarms on nuclear radiation sensors!

1.0079 H HYDROGEN	4.0026 He HELIUM	6.941 Li LITHIUM	9.0122 Be BERYLLIUM	10.811 B BORON	12.011 C CARBON	14.007 N NITROGEN	15.999 O OXYGEN	18.998 F FLUORINE
1	2	3	4	5	6	7	8	9

		B			He	N		
	Be			N			Li	
O			C					B
		F						O
	H			Li			N	
Be						He		
Li					B			Be
	C			H			He	
		He	O			H		

SWING FOR THE FENCE!

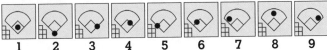

1 2 3 4 5 6 7 8 9

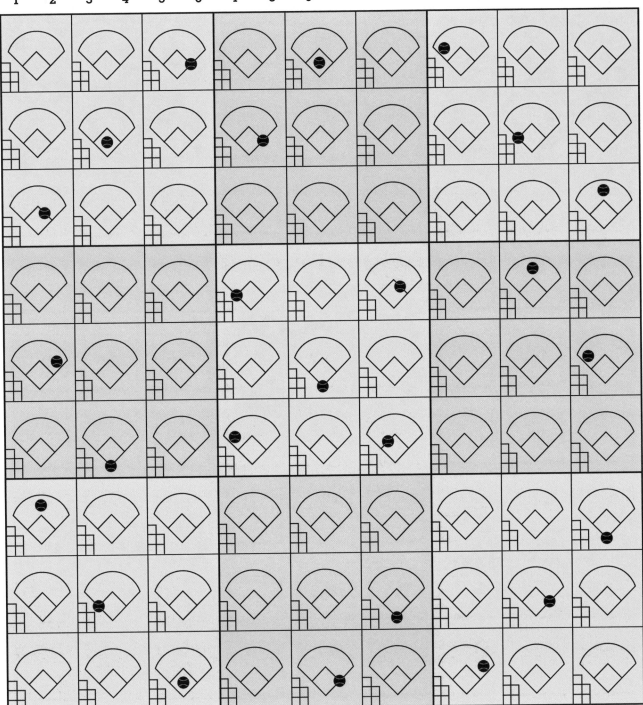

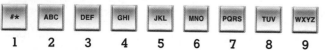

The 411 on 911
In 1967, the number 911 was selected as an emergency number because it was not an area code or the first three numbers in any U.S. or Canadian telephone number.

PLAYING WITH A FULL DECK

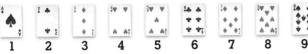

1	2	3	4	5	6	7	8	9

King of Kings
In 16th century Paris, face cards were designed with legendary figures in mind. For example, the King of Spades may be modeled after the biblical King David.

CAST OF CHARACTERS

一	二	三	四	五	六	七	八	九
1	2	3	4	5	6	7	8	9

			九			二		
一				二	四			八
	三						六	
	六		五			七		
七				四				三
		三		一			二	
	五						八	
二			六	九				四
		九		三				

ROCK AROUND THE CLOCK

1 2 3 4 5 6 7 8 9

CARPE SUDOKUM

I	II	III	IV	V	VI	VII	VIII	IX
1	2	3	4	5	6	7	8	9

	VII	IX					IV	VI
		II			VIII			IX
				IX	III			
VIII	II							
VII				V				III
							II	VII
			VI	VIII				
IV			II			IX		
IX	VI						I	III

ALL HAIL BRAILLE

1	2	3	4	5	6	7	8	9

Spies Without Eyes

Braille's six-dot system was inspired by a 12-dot night writing code developed for the French military to send messages that could be read without light on the battlefield.

BRAILLE

GETTING OLD SCHOOLED

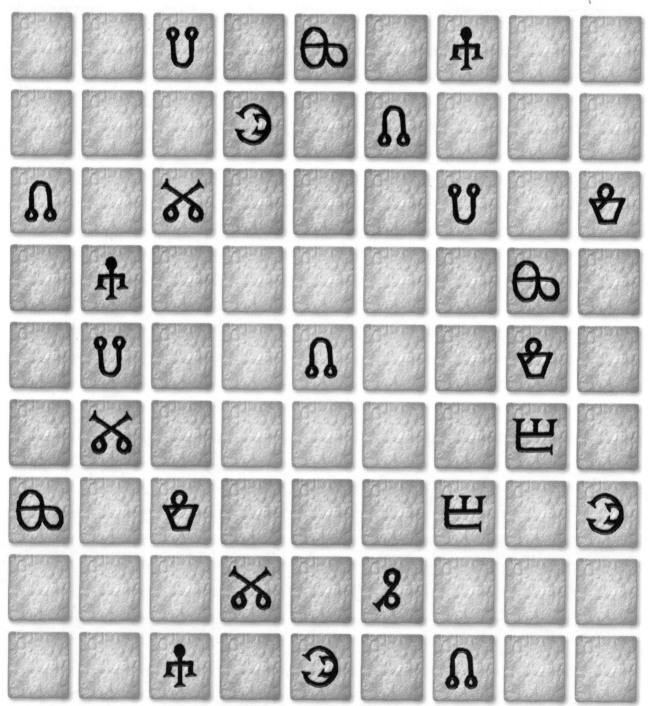

THE DOMINO EFFECT

We All Fall Down
The term "domino theory" derives from an offhanded remark by President Eisenhower in a 1954 speech on the possibility of the spread of communist rule.

WHAT'S YOUR SIGN?

1 2 3 4 5 6 7 8 9

What's the Call?
While experts can't single out the origin of baseball coaching signals, many point to the influence of deaf player Dummy Hoy, whose coach relayed umpire calls to him using hand gestures.

			1	7			4	
	4			4				
1						4	6	
		4	2				1	6
6	6			4				2
4	2					5	2	
	3	3						3
			1				3	
			5	4				

JUST MY TYPE

!	@	#	$	%	∧	&	*	(
1	2	3	4	5	6	7	8	9

Too Little, Too Late
The Dvorak typewriter was considered to have a superior keyboard layout, with the most frequently used keys on the home row, but it arrived too late to the QWERTY party.

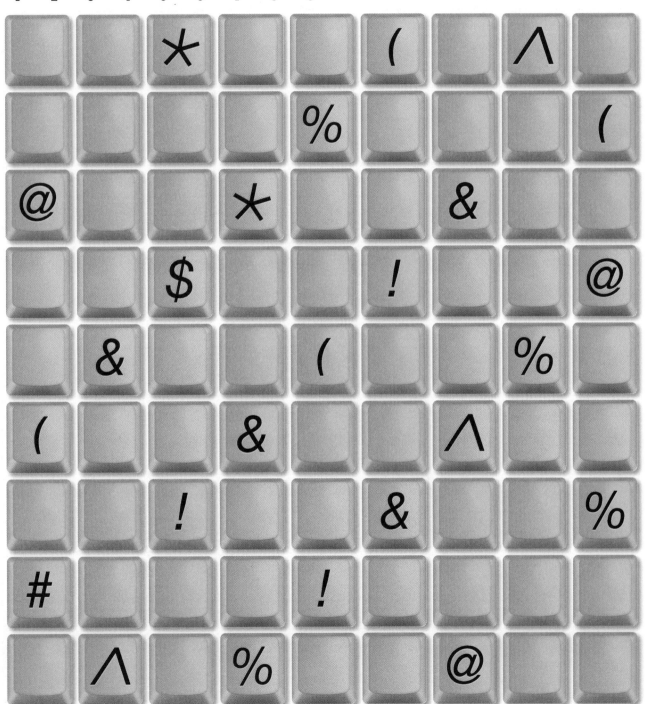

1.0079 H HYDROGEN	4.0026 He HELIUM	6.941 Li LITHIUM	9.0122 Be BERYLLIUM	10.811 B BORON	12.011 C CARBON	14.007 N NITROGEN	15.999 O OXYGEN	18.998 F FLUORINE
1	**2**	**3**	**4**	**5**	**6**	**7**	**8**	**9**

Linguistics of the Table
Some elements at the end of the Periodic Table are given placeholder names (like Ununtrium); when the discovery is verified, the "new" element gets a final name.

1.0079 **H** HYDROGEN	18.998 **F** FLUORINE							6.941 **Li** LITHIUM
		15.999 **O** OXYGEN						14.007 **N** NITROGEN
			1.0079 **H** HYDROGEN		12.011 **C** CARBON		4.0026 **He** HELIUM	
		9.0122 **Be** BERYLLIUM	18.998 **F** FLUORINE		6.941 **Li** LITHIUM	10.811 **B** BORON		
				1.0079 **H** HYDROGEN				
		4.0026 **He** HELIUM	14.007 **N** NITROGEN		15.999 **O** OXYGEN	12.011 **C** CARBON		
	4.0026 **He** HELIUM		9.0122 **Be** BERYLLIUM		10.811 **B** BORON			
9.0122 **Be** BERYLLIUM						6.941 **Li** LITHIUM		
12.011 **C** CARBON							1.0079 **H** HYDROGEN	15.999 **O** OXYGEN

SWING FOR THE FENCE!

1 2 3 4 5 6 7 8 9

Score!
Jimmie Fox and Lou Gehrig share the record for
most consecutive seasons (13) with 100 or more
RBIs (runs batted in).

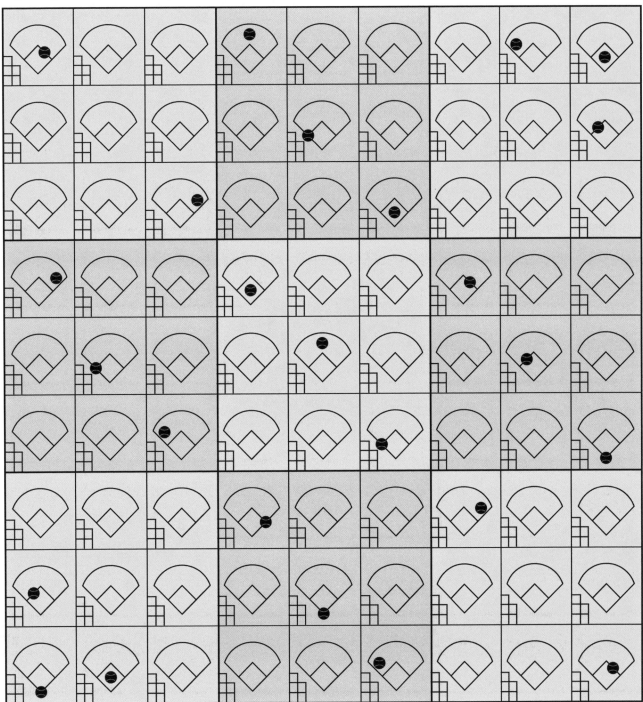

SPEED DIAL

#*	ABC	DEF	GHI	JKL	MNO	PQRS	TUV	WXYZ
1	2	3	4	5	6	7	8	9

No Emergency Here
The first emergency call was placed on February 16, 1968, by Alabama Speaker of the House Rankin Fite to U.S. Representative Tom Bevill at the police station in Hayleyville, Alabama.

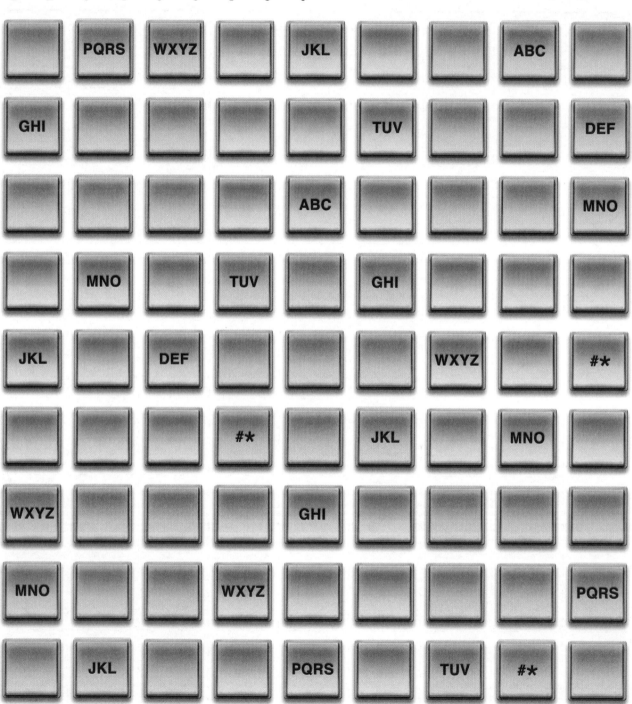

PLAYING WITH A FULL DECK

From Knaves to Kings

A deck of cards is built like the purest of hierarchies, with every card a master to those below it, a lackey to those above it. —Ely Culbertson

CAST OF CHARACTERS

一 二 三 四 五 六 七 八 九
1　2　3　4　5　6　7　8　9

	六		五					九
八			六	三				
				一				
二			九			七	一	
		三		七			五	
		七	八		五			四
			六					
			四	八				七
四					二		三	

ROCK AROUND THE CLOCK

1   2   3   4   5   6   7   8   9

I	II	III	IV	V	VI	VII	VIII	IX
1	2	3	4	5	6	7	8	9

The Lineup
MDCLXVI contains all the Roman numeral letters in order from largest to smallest; when written in Arabic numerals, the number equals 1,666.

MDCLXVI

1	2	3	4	5	6	7	8	9
	VII			IX			VIII	
IX		III			VII			V
				VI			III	
	V					II		
VII				IV				IX
		VI					V	
	II					V		
VI				II		IV		III
	I				III		VI	

ALL HAIL BRAILLE

GETTING OLD SCHOOLED

Ancient Papers
The Kiev Missal, a 10th century Glagolitic canon containing parts of Roman liturgy, is thought to be the oldest manuscript written in coherent Old Church Slavonic text.

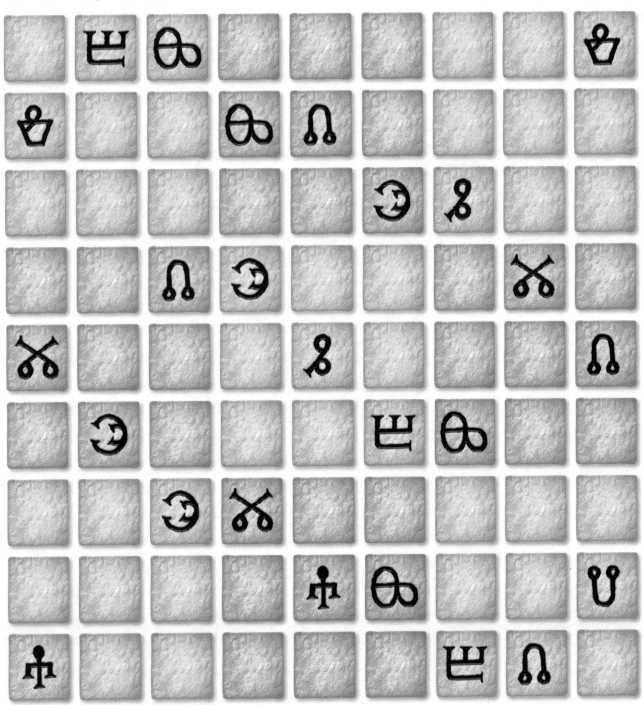

THE DOMINO EFFECT

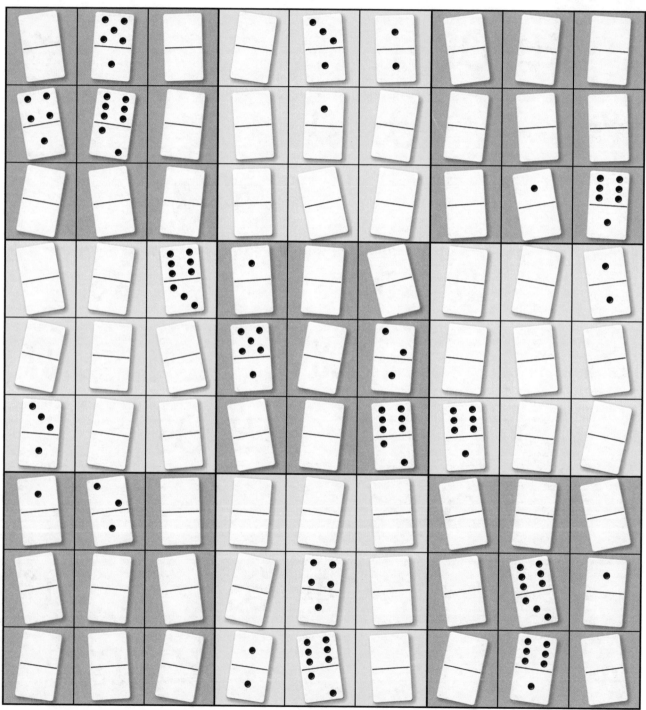

WHAT'S YOUR SIGN?

1 2 3 4 5 6 7 8 9

JUST MY TYPE

!	@	#	$	%	∧	&	✳	(
1	2	3	4	5	6	7	8	9

Expressive Punctuation
Emoticons, called "typographical art," were first published in 1881 in *Puck* magazine. The various emoticons expressed astonishment, indifference, melancholy, and joy.

astonishment   indifference

melancholy   joy

THE ELEMENTS OF STYLE

1.0079	4.0026	6.941	9.0122	10.811	12.011	14.007	15.999	18.998
H	**He**	**Li**	**Be**	**B**	**C**	**N**	**O**	**F**
HYDROGEN	HELIUM	LITHIUM	BERYLLIUM	BORON	CARBON	NITROGEN	OXYGEN	FLUORINE
1	2	3	4	5	6	7	8	9

It's Elementary
Though the Periodic Table of the Elements has been translated into many languages, the symbols of the elements remain universal.

Periodic table of elements

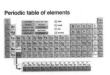

					1.0079 **H** HYDROGEN			
	6.941 **Li** LITHIUM		15.999 **O** OXYGEN			4.0026 **He** HELIUM		
		14.007 **N** NITROGEN	12.011 **C** CARBON			15.999 **O** OXYGEN	10.811 **B** BORON	
	4.0026 **He** HELIUM	9.0122 **Be** BERYLLIUM			18.998 **F** FLUORINE			14.007 **N** NITROGEN
				15.999 **O** OXYGEN				
6.941 **Li** LITHIUM			10.811 **B** BORON			12.011 **C** CARBON	1.0079 **H** HYDROGEN	
	15.999 **O** OXYGEN	10.811 **B** BORON			9.0122 **Be** BERYLLIUM	6.941 **Li** LITHIUM		
		18.998 **F** FLUORINE			14.007 **N** NITROGEN		12.011 **C** CARBON	
			4.0026 **He** HELIUM					

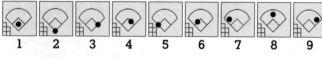

The Bambino
*All ballplayers should quit when it starts to
feel as if the baselines run uphill.*
—Babe Ruth, who retired at age 40

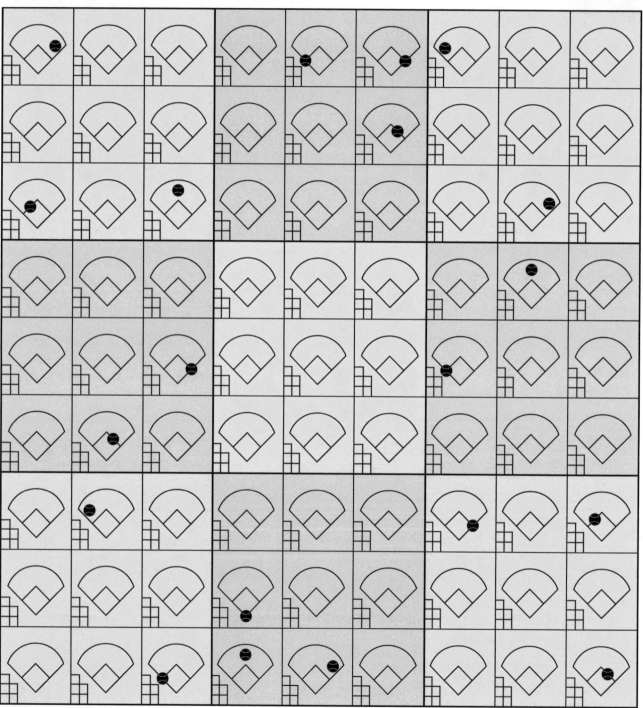

SPEED DIAL

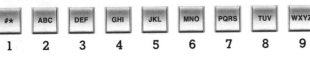

#*	ABC	DEF	GHI	JKL	MNO	PQRS	TUV	WXYZ
1	2	3	4	5	6	7	8	9

Pay to Play
William Gray of Hartford, Connecticut, was the first to patent the coin-operated pay phone. It was installed in a local bank.

		JKL						DEF
			PQRS				GHI	
MNO				#*	WXYZ			
	WXYZ		MNO			ABC		
		TUV				JKL		
		GHI			TUV		MNO	
			TUV	GHI				ABC
	ABC				JKL			
#*						WXYZ		

PLAYING WITH A FULL DECK

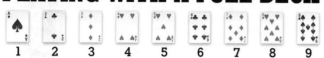

1 A♠ **2** 2♣ **3** 3♦ **4** 4♠ **5** 5♥ **6** 6♣ **7** 7♦ **8** 8♥ **9** 9♠

Always Sit with Your Back to the Wall
Wild Bill Hickok died holding a black pair of Aces and a black pair of Eights, now known as a "Dead Man's Hand." He was shot in the back of the head in his favorite poker haunt.

CAST OF CHARACTERS

一	二	三	四	五	六	七	八	九
1	2	3	4	5	6	7	8	9

All the Single Digits
The name Sudoku (*su* meaning number, *doku* meaning single) is a shortened version of the game's original name, which, translated from the Japanese, means "the digits must be single."

	九	六	四					
五							八	
四			二	一				
八		五	一					
		七			九			
				七	八			一
			三	八				二
	二							三
					九	四	七	

ROCK AROUND THE CLOCK

1 2 3 4 5 6 7 8 9

CARPE SUDOKUM

Out with the Old
The popularity of Roman numerals began to fade when Arab mathematicians introduced Hindu-Arabic numerals to Europe in the 12th century.

I	II	III	IV	V	VI	VII	VIII	IX
1	2	3	4	5	6	7	8	9

	VII					I	VIII	
IX				II				IV
III			I					
		VIII		IV	V			
VI			IX			I		
	VIII	V		VII				
					II			VII
IV				VII				VI
	III	V					IX	

ALL HAIL BRAILLE

1 2 3 4 5 6 7 8 9

A World of Imagination
In her book, *The World I Live In,* Helen Keller described her "dreamland." Her dreams included images, likely because she had sight and hearing when she was very young.

GETTING OLD SCHOOLED

⚜	Ш	ϑ	⅄	Ω	Ϭ	Ж	ꙏ	ꙩ
1	2	3	4	5	6	7	8	9

Back to Earth
The Glagolitic numeral 9, right, corresponds to the alphabet letter Z. It may be related to the Greek *theta*, and means "earth," "ground," or "soil."

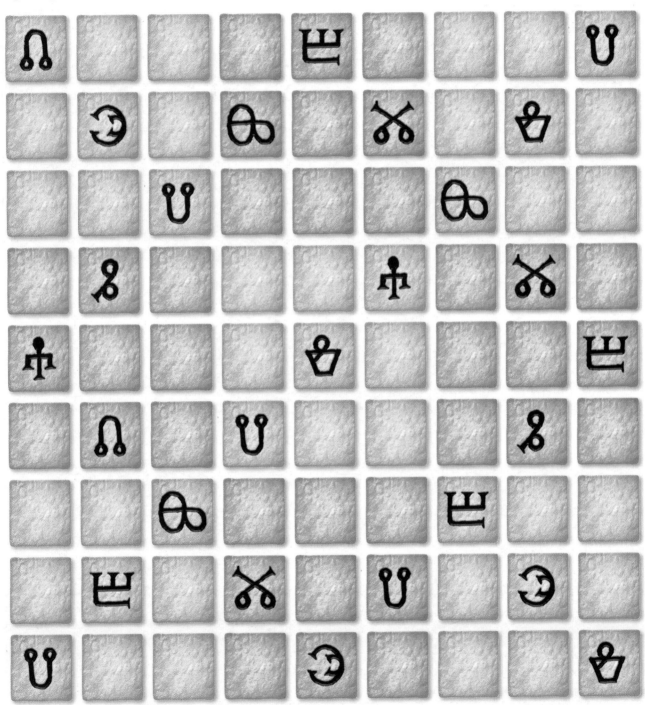

THE DOMINO EFFECT

Scientific Classification of Dominoes
If a domino had four squares on its surface, it would be a tetromino. With five squares, it would be a pentomino—nine, a nonomino, eleven, an unwieldy undecomino!

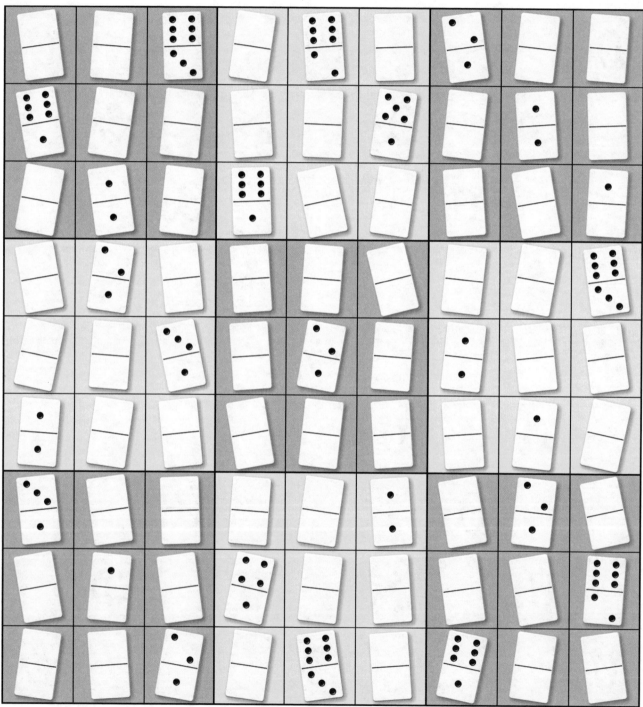

WHAT'S YOUR SIGN?

1 2 3 4 5 6 7 8 9

I Saw the Road Sign
Rochester, New York, has the largest deaf population in the U.S.—90,000 of the area's 700,000 residents are deaf or hearing impaired.

JUST MY TYPE

!	@	#	$	%	∧	&	*	(
1	2	3	4	5	6	7	8	9

The Internet Can Be a Happy Place
In September 1982, Scott Fahlman posted the first "smileys" on the Carnegie Mellon University computer science board, suggesting that :-) and :-(be used to express emotion.

```
:-{}   :'(    :-#   8-)
:-)    :-(    :-/   :-0
:)     :(     :*)   :0
!-)    :-x    ;-)
:'-(   :-D    ;)    @}->--
```

&	(			∧	!			
@					(			
							%	*
		@	(					!
			!		&			
$					#	@		
∧	!							
		#						(
		%	(				*	@

THE ELEMENTS OF STYLE

Silicon Valley Girls
Computer chips start out as beach sand (silicon dioxide), but become semiconductors when they are transformed into single crystals of hyperpure silicon and inscribed with micropatterns.

	14.007 N NITROGEN			10.811 B BORON		15.999 O OXYGEN		
		6.941 Li LITHIUM	1.0079 H HYDROGEN					12.011 C CARBON
10.811 B BORON							1.0079 H HYDROGEN	
			18.998 F FLUORINE		15.999 O OXYGEN		12.011 C CARBON	
14.007 N NITROGEN				1.0079 H HYDROGEN				9.0122 Be BERYLLIUM
	15.999 O OXYGEN		4.0026 He HELIUM		6.941 Li LITHIUM			
	6.941 Li LITHIUM							4.0026 He HELIUM
1.0079 H HYDROGEN					9.0122 Be BERYLLIUM	18.998 F FLUORINE		
		18.998 F FLUORINE		15.999 O OXYGEN			9.0122 Be BERYLLIUM	

SWING FOR THE FENCE!

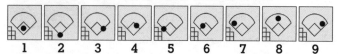

1   2   3   4   5   6   7   8   9

A Real Team Player
St. Louis Cardinal Stan Musial holds the record for most career hits by a player who spent his entire career with the same team—a whopping 3,630.

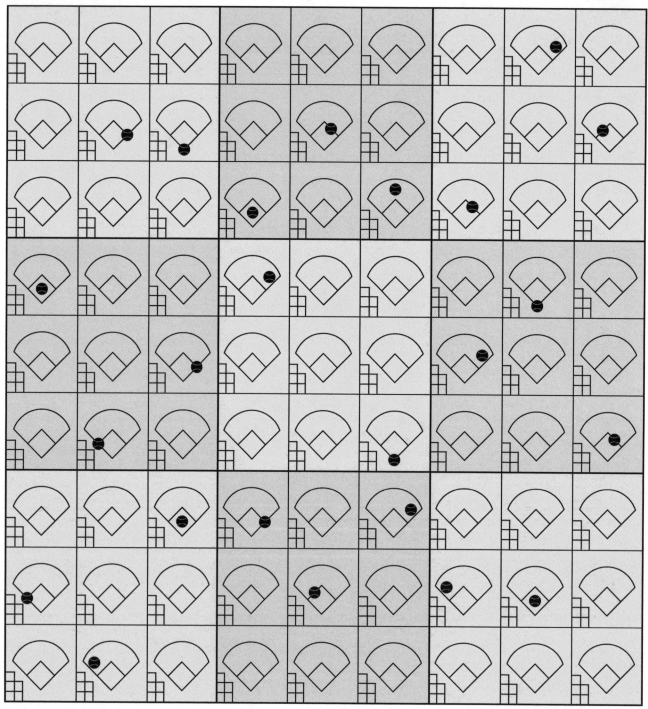

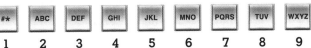

#*	ABC	DEF	GHI	JKL	MNO	PQRS	TUV	WXYZ
1	2	3	4	5	6	7	8	9

The Devil Went Down to Australia
After cartoonist Gary Larson used 555-1332 as Satan's phone number in a cartoon, the owner of the number in Australia (where 555 is an area code) sued Larson for defamation . . . and lost.

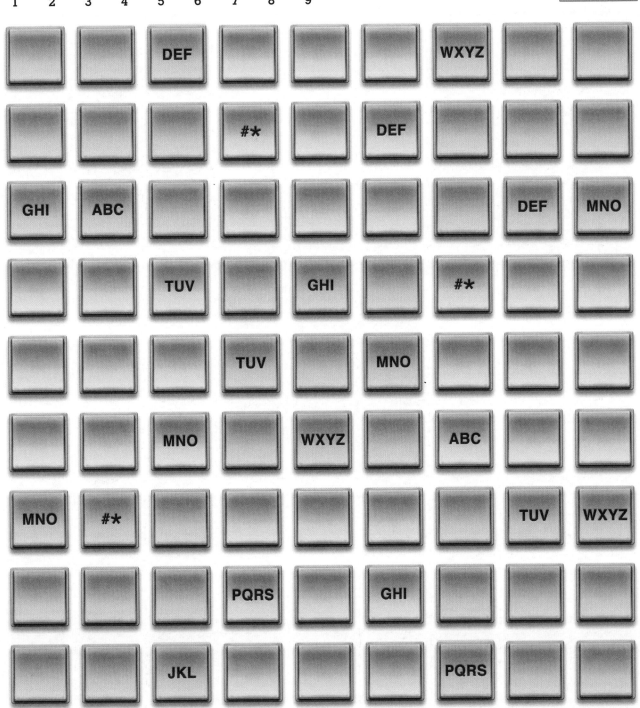

PLAYING WITH A FULL DECK

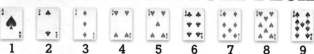

1 2 3 4 5 6 7 8 9

The Windup
Magician Rick Smith, former Cleveland State University baseball pitcher, holds a world record for throwing, or "scaling," a playing card 216 feet and 4 inches.

CAST OF CHARACTERS

一	二	三	四	五	六	七	八	九
1	2	3	4	5	6	7	8	9

						八	二	
			八		七	一		
	三	六					七	四
			六			九	三	
				九				
	二	三				七		
八	九						五	四
				五	一		六	
			七	二				

SUDO-KUBE

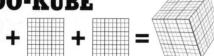

Artistic License
In April 2011, eleven puzzlers from Cube Works Studio in Toronto took more than 400 hours to re-create Michelangelo's *The Hand of God* using a record 12,090 Rubik's Cubes.

ROCK AROUND THE CLOCK

1 2 3 4 5 6 7 8 9

CARPE SUDOKUM

I	II	III	IV	V	VI	VII	VIII	IX
1	2	3	4	5	6	7	8	9

A Rough Few Centuries
Far from impenetrable, Rome was sacked by the Gauls, Visigoths, Vandals, and the Holy Roman Empire between 390 B.C. and A.D. 1527.

	V			IX				VII
III						VII		
		I	II				V	
		III	I					IV
VII				II				VI
	VI				IV	I		
		VI			III	VIII		
			V					III
IV				VI			II	

ALL HAIL BRAILLE

GETTING OLD SCHOOLED

Peace of the Pi
The number 18 in the Glagolitic alphabet may be a variant of the early Greek *pi* (**π**). The corresponding letter P—or "pokoi"—means calmness and peace.

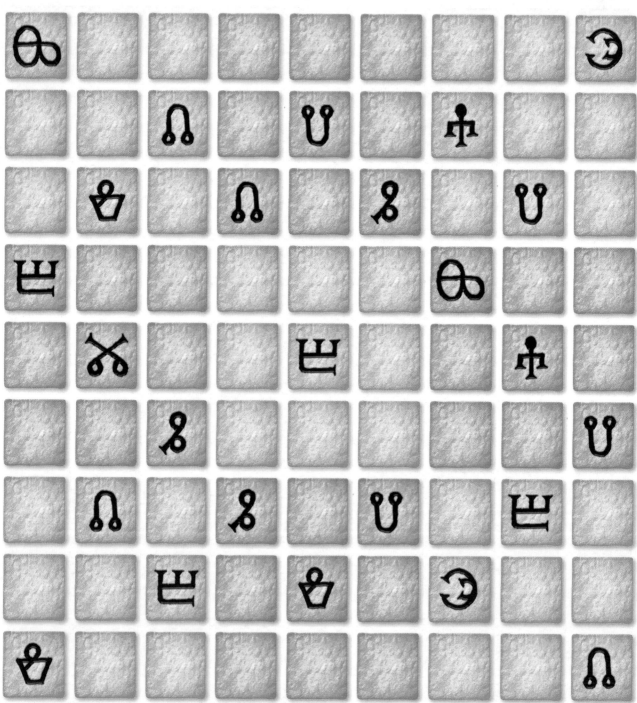

THE DOMINO EFFECT

Expensive Signage
The owners of Domino's Pizza planned to add a dot to the tile on their logo for every new store; but the idea was abandoned after three openings (Domino's now has 9,000 stores worldwide!).

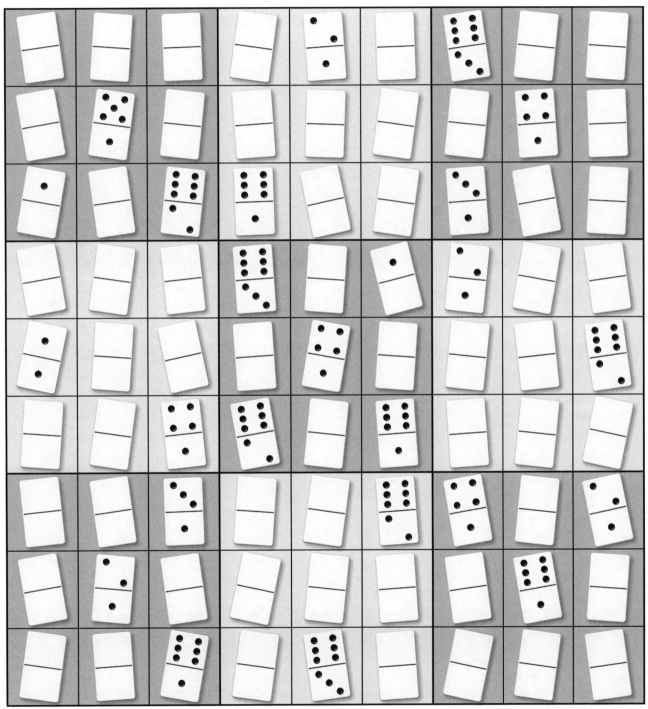

WHAT'S YOUR SIGN?

1 2 3 4 5 6 7 8 9

JUST MY TYPE

Scatterbrained
The first typewriter was designed so that the most common letters or letter combinations (E, T, O, A, H, and N) were scattered as much as possible around the keyboard.

THE ELEMENTS OF STYLE

Brought to You by the Letter J
The letter J is the only letter in the alphabet that never once appears in the Periodic Table.

Key:

1	2	3	4	5	6	7	8	9
1.0079 **H** HYDROGEN	4.0026 **He** HELIUM	6.941 **Li** LITHIUM	9.0122 **Be** BERYLLIUM	10.811 **B** BORON	12.011 **C** CARBON	14.007 **N** NITROGEN	15.999 **O** OXYGEN	18.998 **F** FLUORINE

Puzzle grid:

1	2	3	4	5	6	7	8	9
					He			
		H		N	Be			
		N	C			O	Li	
B	N					C		
	H			F			O	
		Be					F	B
	O	He			H	B		
			Li	Be		He		
			F					

SWING FOR THE FENCE!

1 2 3 4 5 6 7 8 9

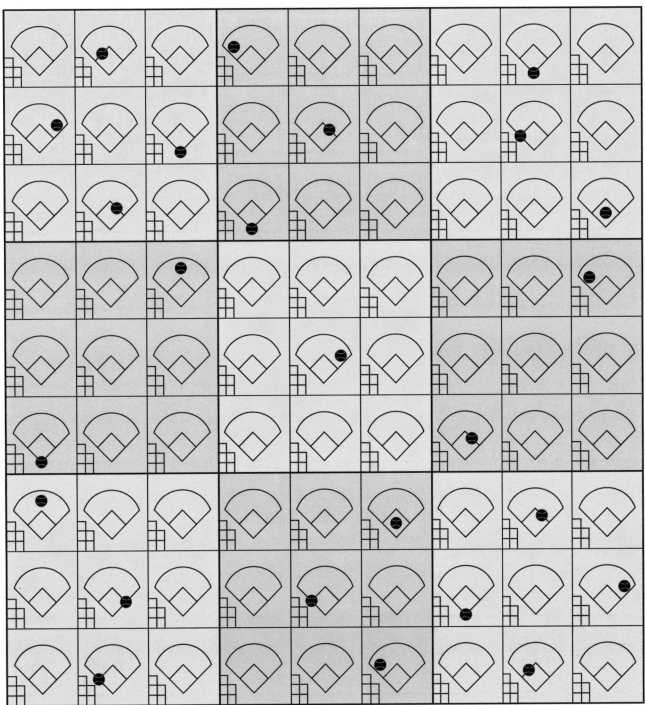

SPEED DIAL

1	2	3	4	5	6	7	8	9
#*	ABC	DEF	GHI	JKL	MNO	PQRS	TUV	WXYZ

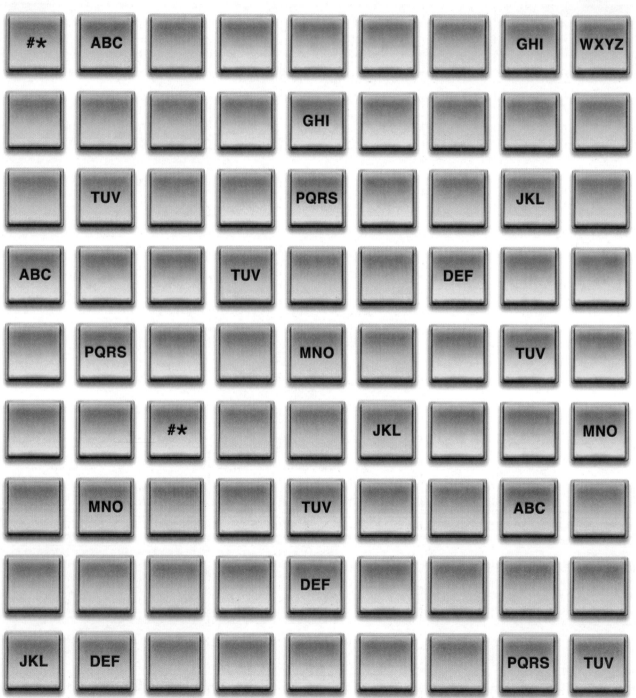

PLAYING WITH A FULL DECK

Suit Yourself
The international deck, with suits of coins, goblets, polo sticks, and swords, evolved in Europe from the 52-card Mamlūk deck.

CAST OF CHARACTERS

一	二	三	四	五	六	七	八	九
1	2	3	4	5	6	7	8	9

Imported Art
Japanese calligraphy developed when sets of written Chinese characters (*kanji*) were introduced alongside Buddhism and Confucianism in the sixth century.

美丽　永恒　生命
混乱　诺言　爱
勇气　家庭　幸运
死亡　友谊　和平
命运　欢喜　力量
梦想　希望　智慧
热情　变化　真相

八					六			一
	四	六		三				七
			五				二	
		三	七			二	四	
		三				二		
	九				五			
	一			八				
二				六		一	九	
五			二					六

ROCK AROUND THE CLOCK

1 2 3 4 5 6 7 8 9

CARPE SUDOKUM

Roman Redux
Rome Reborn, an interactive site sponsored by the University of Virginia, offers a 3-D digital model of ancient Rome circa A.D. 320.

| I | II | III | IV | V | VI | VII | VIII | IX |
| 1 | 2 | 3 | 4 | 5 | 6 | 7 | 8 | 9 |

I	II	III	IV	V	VI	VII	VIII	IX
V				VII	VIII			
IV								
			II	IV			VIII	I
			I	VI			V	VIII
VII	IV				II	IX		
II	VIII				VII	IV		
								IX
			VIII	I				VI

140 🏠 MEDIUM

ALL HAIL BRAILLE

1 2 3 4 5 6 7 8 9

I Feel It in My Fingers
The fingertips have more nerve endings than most other parts of the body. Each fingertip has an estimated 3,000 touch receptors!

GETTING OLD SCHOOLED

ⴀ ⴁ ⴂ ⴃ ⴄ ⴅ ⴆ ⴇ ⴈ
1 2 3 4 5 6 7 8 9

Talking in Circles
Glagolitic numeral 4 translates to *glagoli*, which is the root of the numeric alphabet's name and means "to do" or, most aptly, "to speak."

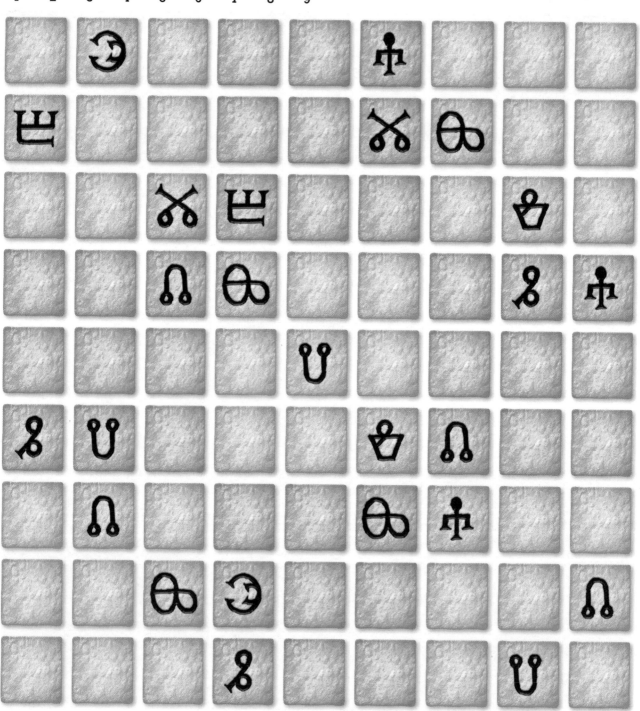

THE DOMINO EFFECT

Oh, Lord.
The word "domino" probably derives from the latin *dominus*, meaning lord or master.

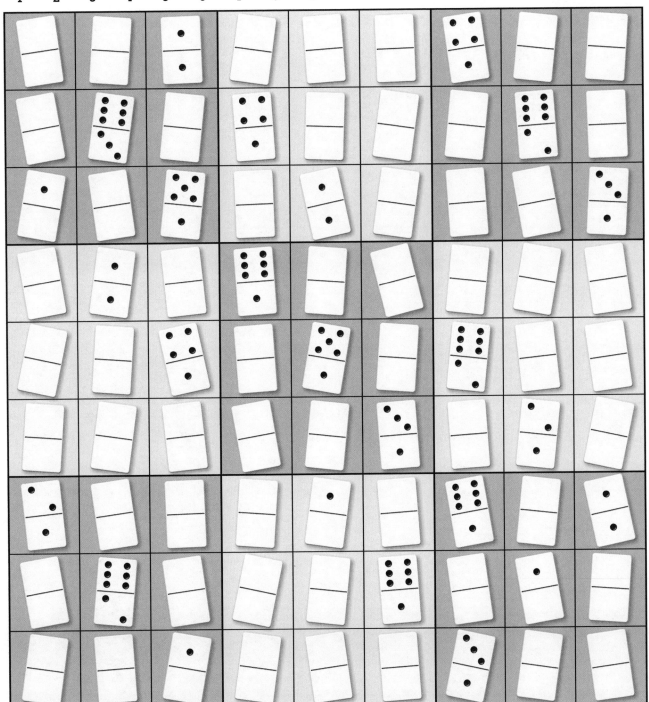

WHAT'S YOUR SIGN?

1 2 3 4 5 6 7 8 9

Poetic Phalanges

In sign language poetry, you can sign a poem by "rhyming" words whose signs share a similar hand shape and motion or by repeating others.

JUST MY TYPE

Show-Offs

Remington engineers modified the keys on their typewriter model so that salesmen could show off their machines by writing the word "typewriter" quickly. All of the letters are in the top row.

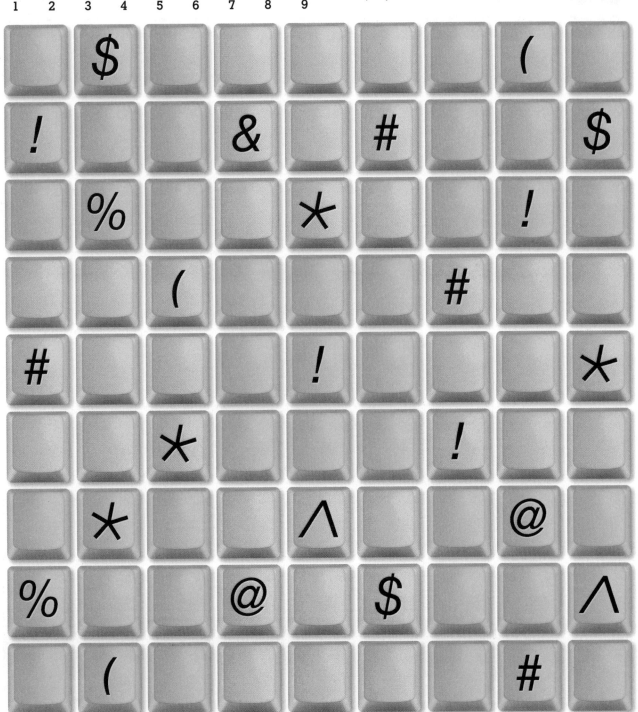

1.0079	4.0026	6.941	9.0122	10.811	12.011	14.007	15.999	18.998
H	He	Li	Be	B	C	N	O	F
HYDROGEN	HELIUM	LITHIUM	BERYLLIUM	BORON	CARBON	NITROGEN	OXYGEN	FLUORINE
1	2	3	4	5	6	7	8	9

Barely There
Astatine is the rarest occurring element found in nature. It's estimated that fewer than 50 milligrams of astatine can be found in the top kilometer of the earth's crust.

	14.007 N NITROGEN			6.941 Li LITHIUM			12.011 C CARBON	
10.811 B BORON					12.011 C CARBON			9.0122 Be BERYLLIUM
		4.0026 He HELIUM					18.998 F FLUORINE	
	6.941 Li LITHIUM			14.007 N NITROGEN				18.998 F FLUORINE
18.998 F FLUORINE							14.007 N NITROGEN	
4.0026 He HELIUM				12.011 C CARBON		10.811 B BORON		
	4.0026 He HELIUM				15.999 O OXYGEN			
1.0079 H HYDROGEN		9.0122 Be BERYLLIUM						6.941 Li LITHIUM
	12.011 C CARBON			1.0079 H HYDROGEN			4.0026 He HELIUM	

SWING FOR THE FENCE!

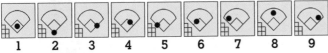

1 2 3 4 5 6 7 8 9

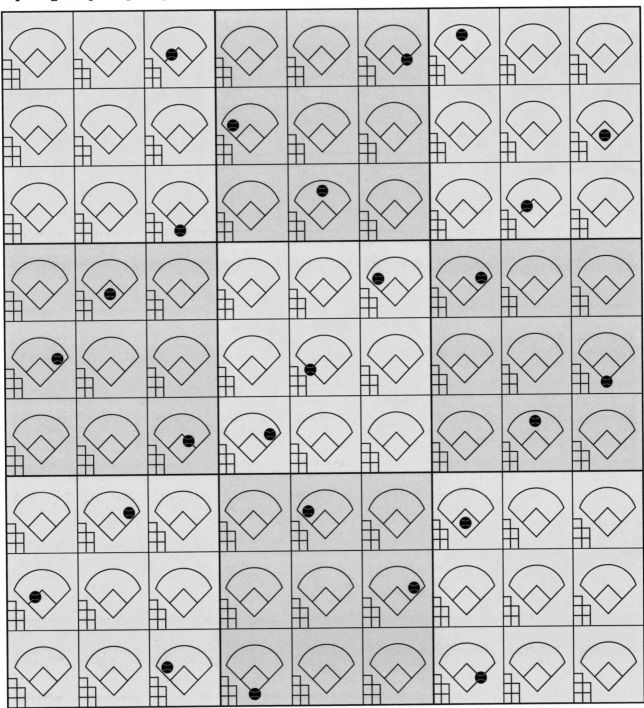

SPEED DIAL

#*	ABC	DEF	GHI	JKL	MNO	PQRS	TUV	WXYZ
1	2	3	4	5	6	7	8	9

High Stakes Texting
The fastest texter on record is Cheong Kit Au of Australia, who typed a 264-character text in 1 minute, 17.03 seconds during the 2011 LG Mobile World Cup in New York.

	DEF			PQRS			GHI	
JKL	PQRS					WXYZ		MNO
						#*		
			WXYZ		GHI		ABC	
WXYZ			#*					PQRS
	TUV		PQRS		MNO			
	ABC							
DEF			ABC				WXYZ	JKL
	#*		JKL				DEF	

PLAYING WITH A FULL DECK

1 2 3 4 5 6 7 8 9

CAST OF CHARACTERS

一	二	三	四	五	六	七	八	九
1	2	3	4	5	6	7	8	9

A *Kanji* Is Worth 1,000 *Kana*
Kana, phonetic Japanese characters, evolved from the process of adapting Chinese characters (*kanji*, pictograms) to the Japanese language. Both *kanji* and *kana* are used in calligraphy.

		二					一	
	八			五				二
五				九		四	六	
				三				四
			八				二	
	九					七		
			五	四		二		一
八				六			九	
	三					四		

SUDO-KUBE

ROCK AROUND THE CLOCK

1 2 3 4 5 6 7 8 9

Battling the Clock
From February 9, 1942, to September 30, 1945 (during World War II), clocks were kept an entire hour ahead in the United States, in what was called "Eastern War Time."

CARPE SUDOKUM

I	II	III	IV	V	VI	VII	VIII	IX
1	2	3	4	5	6	7	8	9

IV							VI	VIII
	VIII		V	IX				VII
					VII			
			III			VIII	II	
	VI						V	
	IV	VIII			VI			
			I					
V			IV	IX			I	
VIII	IX							III

ALL HAIL BRAILLE

1 2 3 4 5 6 7 8 9

The First and Last Sense

In embryos, the sense of touch develops before all others and continues to function in old age, long after the other four senses begin to fail or become less effective.

GETTING OLD SCHOOLED

Everything Is Illuminated
The Hrvoje's Missal, a liturgical text written in 1404, is considered one of the most remarkable illuminated Glagolitic manuscripts.

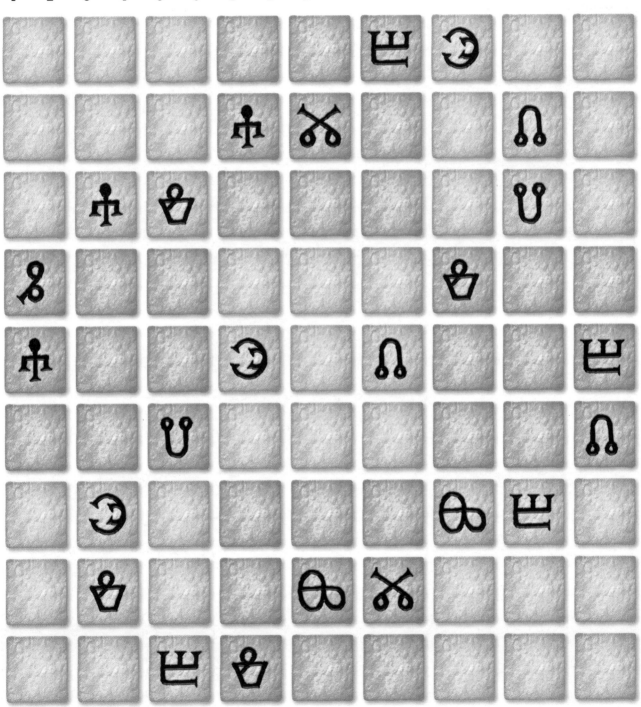

THE DOMINO EFFECT

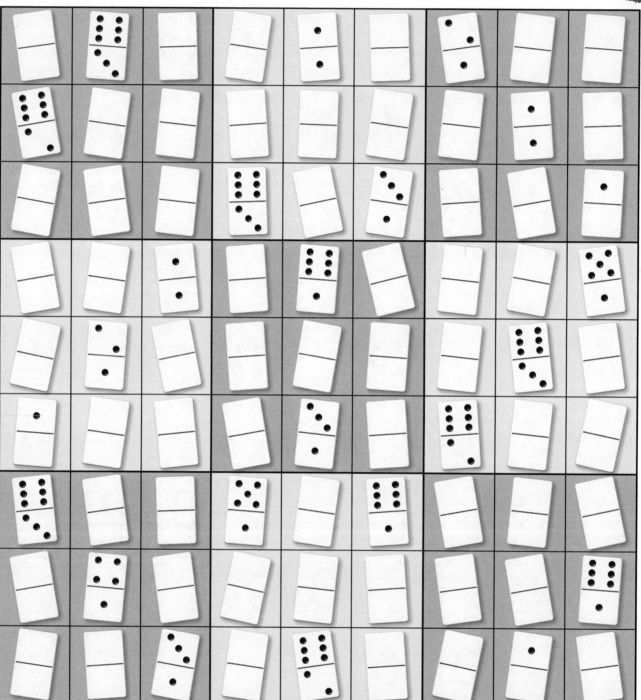

Bye Bye, Birdie
A sparrow nearly foiled a world-record attempt when it knocked over 23,000 dominoes in Leeuwarden, Netherlands. Luckily, the other 3 million-plus in the chain remained standing.

WHAT'S YOUR SIGN?

1 2 3 4 5 6 7 8 9

JUST MY TYPE

!	@	#	$	%	∧	&	∗	(
1	2	3	4	5	6	7	8	9

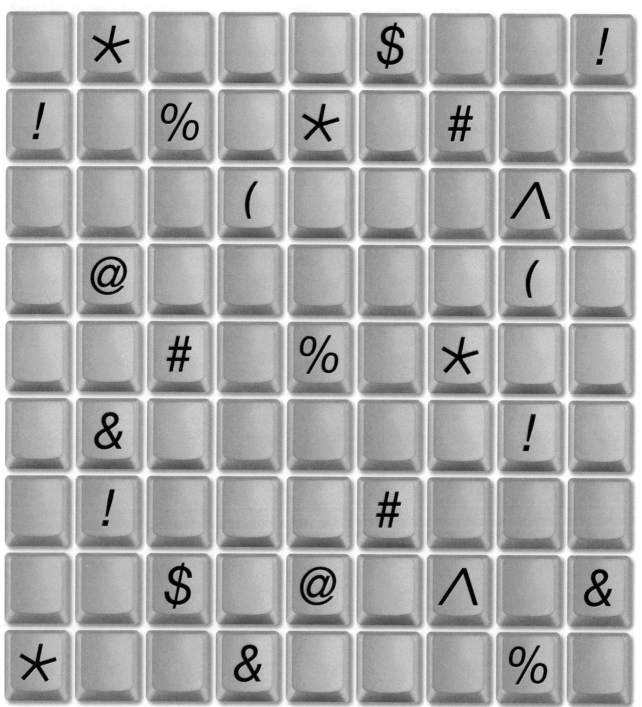

THE ELEMENTS OF STYLE

Fake It Till You Make It
Technetium was the first element to be produced artificially, isolated by Carlo Perrier and Emilio Segrè in their laboratory. Its name comes from the Greek *technetos,* for "artificial."

			He 4.0026 HELIUM					
	H 1.0079 HYDROGEN	F 18.998 FLUORINE		Li 6.941 LITHIUM				
	N 14.007 NITROGEN				H 1.0079 HYDROGEN	O 15.999 OXYGEN		
B 10.811 BORON				He 4.0026 HELIUM		H 1.0079 HYDROGEN		
	O 15.999 OXYGEN		B 10.811 BORON		N 14.007 NITROGEN		Li 6.941 LITHIUM	
		Be 9.0122 BERYLLIUM		C 12.011 CARBON				O 15.999 OXYGEN
		Li 6.941 LITHIUM	O 15.999 OXYGEN				H 1.0079 HYDROGEN	
				H 1.0079 HYDROGEN		N 14.007 NITROGEN	F 18.998 FLUORINE	
					C 12.011 CARBON			

SWING FOR THE FENCE!

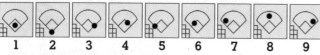

1 2 3 4 5 6 7 8 9

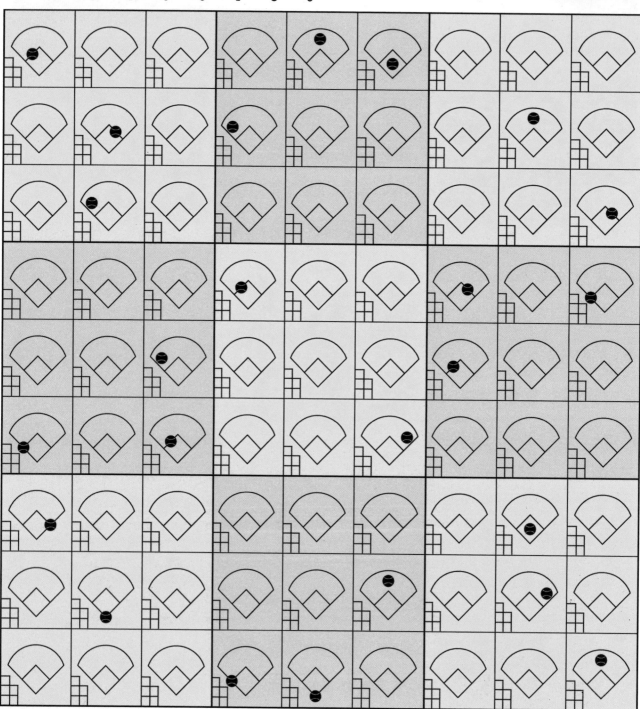

SPEED DIAL

#*	ABC	DEF	GHI	JKL	MNO	PQRS	TUV	WXYZ
1	2	3	4	5	6	7	8	9

Just Send Me a TXT MSG
Acronyms are the fastest way to send info-rich messages: ASAMOF, I'm ROTFL and TTKASF says, "As a matter of fact, I'm rolling on the floor laughing and trying to keep a straight face."

	MNO			PQRS	JKL			
ABC						PQRS		
#*						JKL		MNO
	PQRS	#*						GHI
			WXYZ	GHI	#*			
WXYZ						#*	DEF	
JKL		WXYZ						#*
		ABC						DEF
		ABC	JKL				MNO	

PLAYING WITH A FULL DECK

1 **2** **3** **4** **5** **6** **7** **8** **9**

All Decked Out
The longest poker game was recorded in June 2010 in Las Vegas and added up to over 115 hours of live poker. The winner, Phil Laak, netted $6,766 and donated half to charity.

Vertical Leap
Japanese books are typically written using vertical writing, or *tategaki,* and are read right to left across the page.

	七						九	
六			三		七			一
	四		六					
	三		九				一	
			一	二		八		
	二				一	五		
			七		三			
九			八	六				二
	一						七	

ROCK AROUND THE CLOCK

1   2   3   4   5   6   7   8   9

A Wrinkle in Time . . .
Paul Harding's Pulitzer Prize–winning novel, *Tinkers,* follows an aging clock repairer, in his final moments, as he wanders through time and in and out of consciousness.

CARPE SUDOKUM

I	II	III	IV	V	VI	VII	VIII	IX
1	2	3	4	5	6	7	8	9

The Remains of an Empire
Beyond Roman numerals, the cultural legacy of the Roman Empire extends to Romance languages, the Western alphabet, and the 12-month calendar.

			VI				V	
		I		VI				II
II					III		VIII	
IX			I			VIII		
	III			V			I	
		V			VIII			IV
	IX			VI				I
VII					IX		III	
		II				VI		

ALL HAIL BRAILLE

1 2 3 4 5 6 7 8 9

Snuggle Up
The sense of touch, which supports a newborn's cognitive development by facilitating emotional bonds, is the primary way that infants learn about the world around them.

GETTING OLD SCHOOLED

THE DOMINO EFFECT

The Name, Not the Game
After Hurricane Katrina, prominent local musician Fats Domino made a surprise appearance at a namesake concert, The Domino Effect, which raised money to rebuild schools.

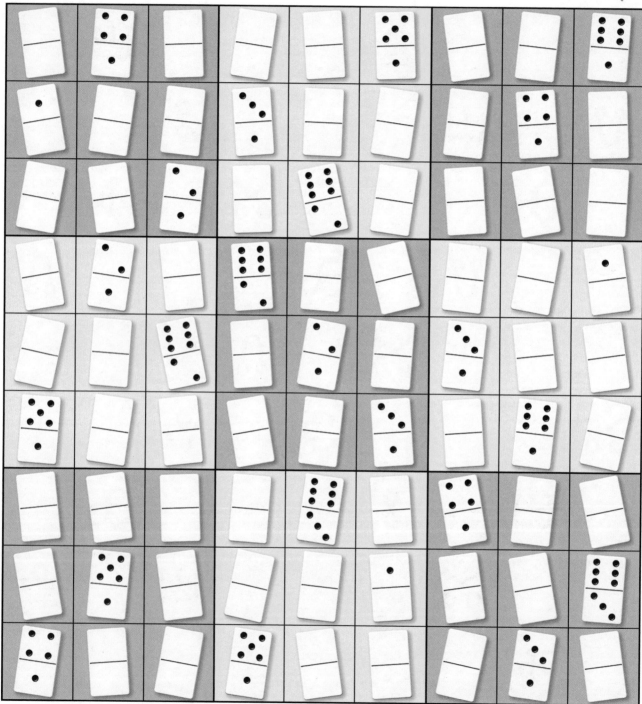

168 🏠 MEDIUM

WHAT'S YOUR SIGN?

1 2 3 4 5 6 7 8 9

		7			9			1
	7			2			8	
2			4			7		
	4						5	
	5		2		5			
	7				7			9
	5			8			4	
	2		2			4		
4		8			5			

JUST MY TYPE

!	@	#	$	%	∧	&	✳	(
1	2	3	4	5	6	7	8	9

Hunt and Peck
In the early years of typewriters, eight-finger typing was unheard of—proficient typists could type 20 or 30 words per minute, which was about the rate of handwriting.

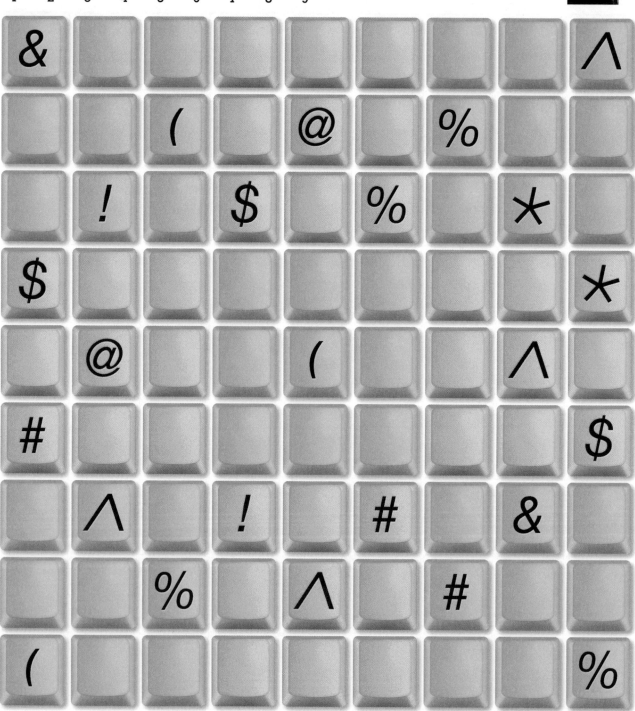

THE ELEMENTS OF STYLE

1.0079 H HYDROGEN	4.0026 He HELIUM	6.941 Li LITHIUM	9.0122 Be BERYLLIUM	10.811 B BORON	12.011 C CARBON	14.007 N NITROGEN	15.999 O OXYGEN	18.998 F FLUORINE
1	2	3	4	5	6	7	8	9

Bath Bomb
When highly reactive alkali metals, like sodium and francium (which can't be found in their elemental forms in nature), are exposed to water, they create an explosion.

		18.998 F FLUORINE			14.007 N NITROGEN	9.0122 Be BERYLLIUM		
	12.011 C CARBON			10.811 B BORON			4.0026 He HELIUM	
9.0122 Be BERYLLIUM					12.011 C CARBON			14.007 N NITROGEN
						12.011 C CARBON		4.0026 He HELIUM
	18.998 F FLUORINE			14.007 N NITROGEN			15.999 O OXYGEN	
10.811 B BORON		1.0079 H HYDROGEN						
15.999 O OXYGEN			6.941 Li LITHIUM					1.0079 H HYDROGEN
	10.811 B BORON			1.0079 H HYDROGEN			6.941 Li LITHIUM	
		12.011 C CARBON	9.0122 Be BERYLLIUM			10.811 B BORON		

SWING FOR THE FENCE!

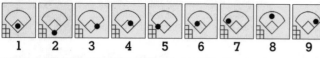

1 2 3 4 5 6 7 8 9

Base Burglar
Honus Wagner, whose baseball card is the most expensive in the world, is the only National League player to steal his way from first to home five times in a career.

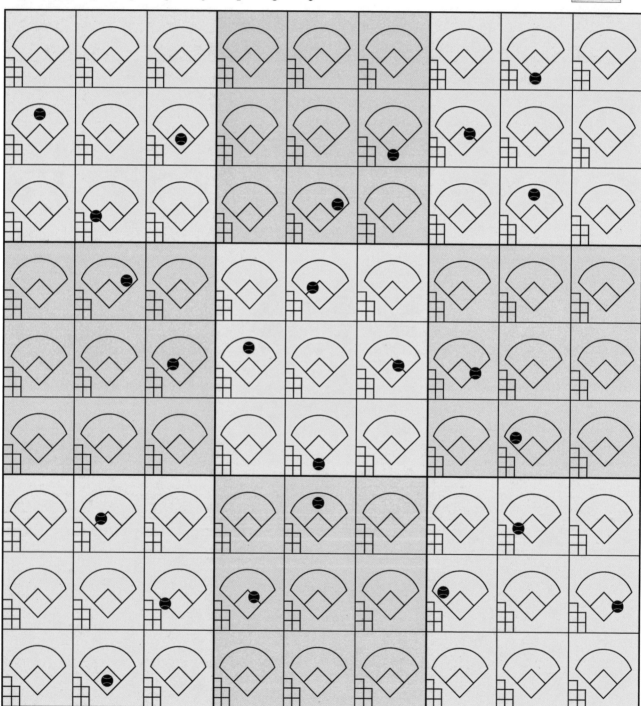

SPEED DIAL

Please Press 9 for WINNING
In 1973, Martin Cooper, the father of the mobile phone, placed the first call on his cellular Motorola device to Bell Labs, the company competing to create a portable phone.

	TUV						WXYZ	
		WXYZ		#*		ABC		
GHI			WXYZ		MNO			DEF
		#*				JKL		
	WXYZ			GHI			MNO	
		ABC				PQRS		
WXYZ			#*		PQRS			ABC
		TUV		DEF		GHI		
	ABC						PQRS	

PLAYING WITH A FULL DECK

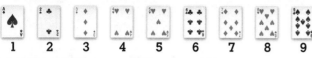

1 2 3 4 5 6 7 8 9

CAST OF CHARACTERS

一	二	三	四	五	六	七	八	九
1	2	3	4	5	6	7	8	9

The Way of Japan
Calligraphy is *shodo* in Japanese, meaning "the way of writing." The translation is similar to *chado*, "the way of tea" and *kado*, "the way of flowers," both important cultural rituals.

三					九			
二				五				九
	一			七				五
			二		八		七	
			七				八	
		八	五				二	
五				八			九	
六					四			一
				六				二

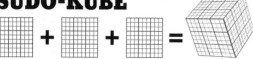

ROCK AROUND THE CLOCK

1   2   3   4   5   6   7   8   9

A Renewed Sense of Time

An estimated one million people stand in Times Square each New Year's Eve to watch the ball drop and the clock count down to ring in the new year.

CARPE SUDOKUM

I (1) II (2) III (3) IV (4) V (5) VI (6) VII (7) VIII (8) IX (9)

1	2	3	4	5	6	7	8	9
		VIII		I	II			
		III	IX					
IX	IV				III			
	VIII					I		VI
V				IV				VIII
VI		II					IX	
			IV				III	IX
					VI	V		
			I	VIII		VI		

ALL HAIL BRAILLE

1 2 3 4 5 6 7 8 9

Complete with Raised Dots
In 2009, on the 200th anniversary of Braille's birth, Belgium and Italy minted two euro coins, India created a two-rupee coin, and the U.S. issued a dollar coin in celebration.

GETTING OLD SCHOOLED

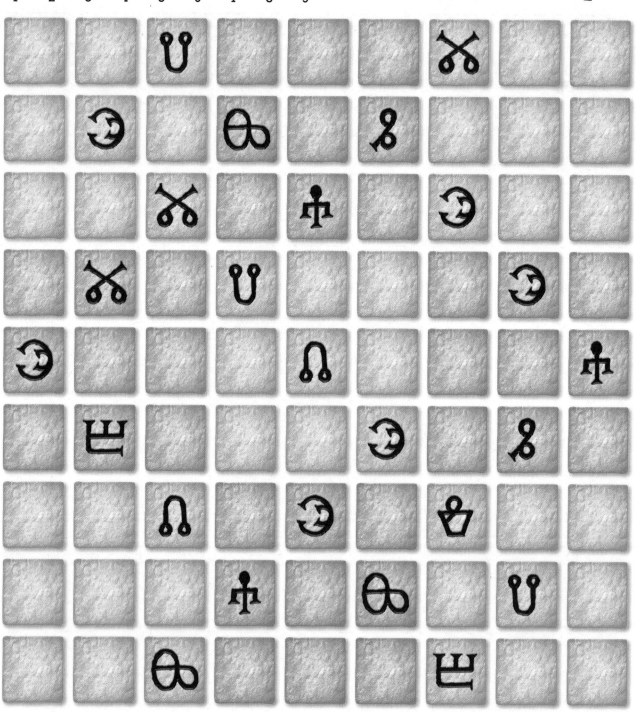

Square One
The first number in the Glagolitic alphabet means "I." It also corresponds with the letter A and the Phoenician *aleph*, or the sign of the cross.

THE DOMINO EFFECT

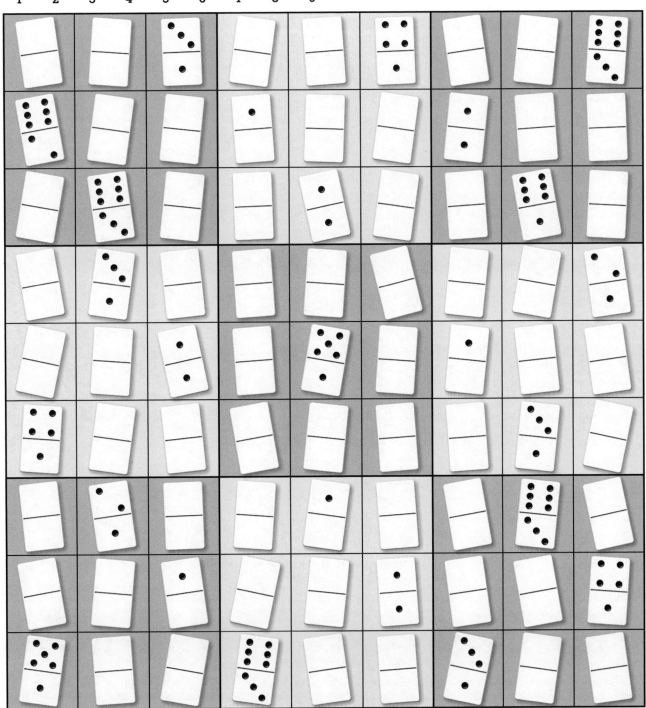

A Sweet Marketing Plan
Brothers William and Frederick Havemeyer rebranded their refined product "Domino Sugar" at the turn of the 20th century because the sugar cubes were said to resemble dominoes.

MEDIUM 🏠 181

WHAT'S YOUR SIGN?

1 2 3 4 5 6 7 8 9

Born This Way
According to the Deafness Research Foundation, loss of hearing is the most prevalent sensory loss in the U.S. In fact, 1 in 1,000 babies is born deaf.

JUST MY TYPE

Accepted for Publication
The first typewritten manuscript ever to be submitted to a publisher was *The Adventures of Tom Sawyer*, which Mark Twain typed on a Remington typewriter he purchased in 1874.

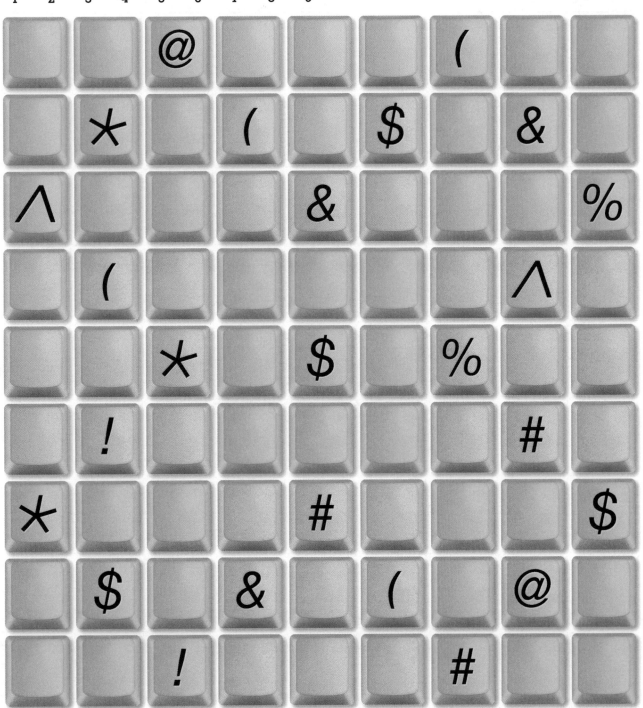

THE ELEMENTS OF STYLE

| 1.0079 H HYDROGEN 1 | 4.0026 He HELIUM 2 | 6.941 Li LITHIUM 3 | 9.0122 Be BERYLLIUM 4 | 10.811 B BORON 5 | 12.011 C CARBON 6 | 14.007 N NITROGEN 7 | 15.999 O OXYGEN 8 | 18.998 F FLUORINE 9 |

A Coppertone Goddess
Copper derives its name from the Latin word *cyprium,* after the island of Cyprus, where the metal was mined in Roman times; the element was associated with Venus, goddess of love and beauty.

	15.999 O OXYGEN						10.811 B BORON	
	14.007 N NITROGEN			1.0079 H HYDROGEN				12.011 C CARBON
	18.998 F FLUORINE		12.011 C CARBON			9.0122 Be BERYLLIUM		
14.007 N NITROGEN		6.941 Li LITHIUM			18.998 F FLUORINE			
	12.011 C CARBON		9.0122 Be BERYLLIUM			4.0026 He HELIUM		
	4.0026 He HELIUM			10.811 B BORON				14.007 N NITROGEN
	14.007 N NITROGEN		1.0079 H HYDROGEN			12.011 C CARBON		
4.0026 He HELIUM		10.811 B BORON			9.0122 Be BERYLLIUM			
	1.0079 H HYDROGEN					6.941 Li LITHIUM		

SWING FOR THE FENCE!

1 2 3 4 5 6 7 8 9

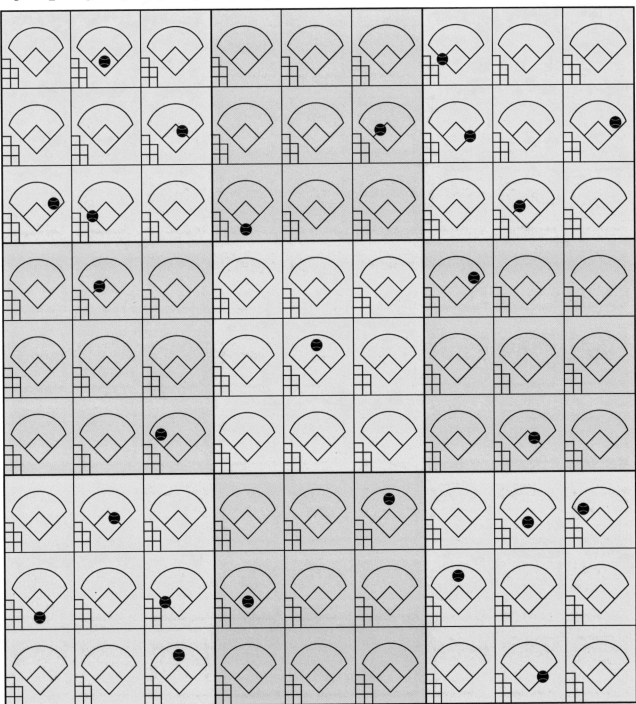

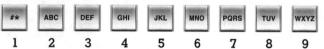

#*	ABC	DEF	GHI	JKL	MNO	PQRS	TUV	WXYZ
1	2	3	4	5	6	7	8	9

Oh My God, Becky . . .
The 1992 number one single "Baby Got Back" is well-known for the number in its lyrics, 1-900-MIX-A LOT, a set of digits riffing on the artist's name.

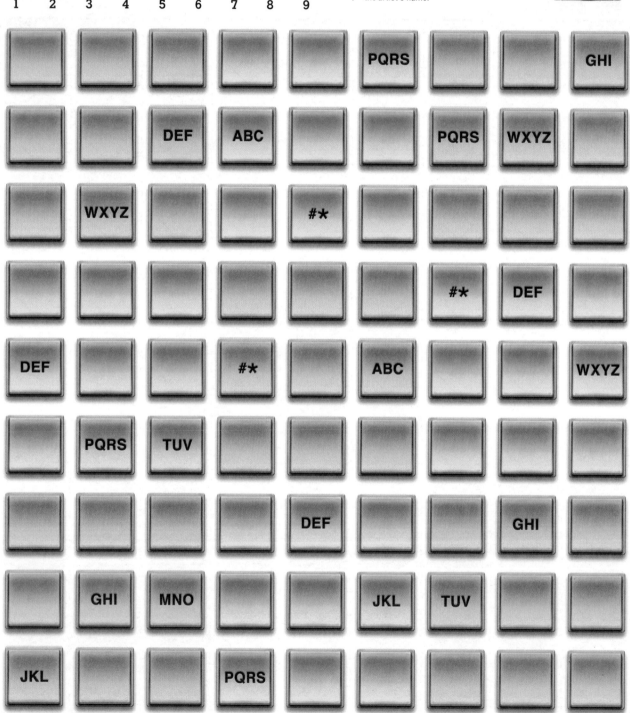

PLAYING WITH A FULL DECK

All Hands on Deck
The best poker hands are, in order: Royal Flush, Straight Flush, Four-of-a-Kind, Full House, Flush, Straight, Three-of-a-Kind, Two Pair, and One Pair.

CAST OF CHARACTERS

一	二	三	四	五	六	七	八	九
1	2	3	4	5	6	7	8	9

Be the Brush

Zen in its essence is the art of seeing into the nature of one's being, and it points the way from bondage to freedom. —**D. T. Suzuki**

一		五		七				八
三					五			二
	九				一			
	二					三		
		七		三		二		
		三					四	
				三			九	
八				九				六
九				六		五		一

ROCK AROUND THE CLOCK

1 2 3 4 5 6 7 8 9

CARPE SUDOKUM

Rated IIB

In Hong Kong, the system used to classify and rate a film's content includes Roman numeral–based categories.

I	II	III	IV	V	VI	VII	VIII	IX
1	2	3	4	5	6	7	8	9

						IV		II
			IX	II		VII		
VII	V				I			IX
		III					V	
IX				V				VIII
	VIII					IV		
III			V				II	I
		IV			IX	III		
VIII				III				

190 MEDIUM

ALL HAIL BRAILLE

1 2 3 4 5 6 7 8 9

Paper Savers
Most books in Braille are embossed on just one side of the page, but books using Interpoint Braille are double-sided—the rows of cells are staggered to avoid interference.

GETTING OLD SCHOOLED

Religious Rebels
In A.D. 886, when Glagolitic script was banned, 200 followers of its creator, Methodius, were jailed as slaves; others became clergymen in other countries and spread the alphabet further.

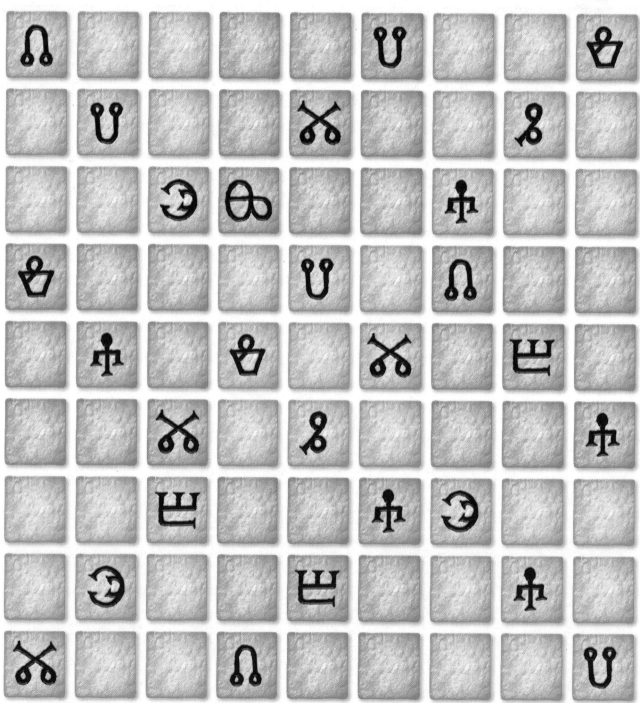

THE DOMINO EFFECT

WHAT'S YOUR SIGN?

 1 2 3 4 5 6 7 8 9

Man and Machine
Many in the deaf and hard of hearing community worry that hearing devices like the cochlear implant could jeopardize the American Sign Language tradition.

JUST MY TYPE

!	@	#	$	%	∧	&	∗	(
1	2	3	4	5	6	7	8	9

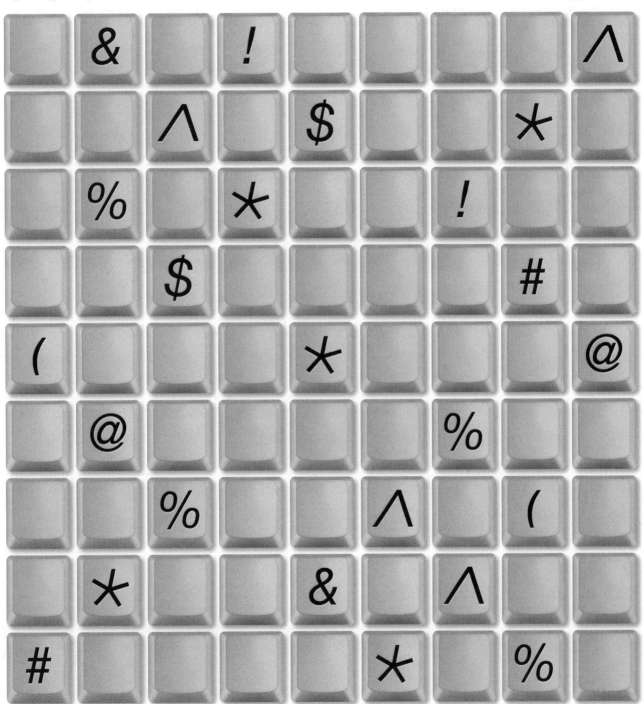

THE ELEMENTS OF STYLE

1.0079 H HYDROGEN	4.0026 He HELIUM	6.941 Li LITHIUM	9.0122 Be BERYLLIUM	10.811 B BORON	12.011 C CARBON	14.007 N NITROGEN	15.999 O OXYGEN	18.998 F FLUORINE
1	2	3	4	5	6	7	8	9

It's Everyday and Out of this World!
Beryllium, an element one-third lighter than aluminum, yet six times as stiff as steel, can be found in cell phones and kitchen appliances, as well as in space shuttles and telescopes.

1	2	3	4	5	6	7	8	9
					14.007 N NITROGEN		12.011 C CARBON	
10.811 B BORON			12.011 C CARBON			1.0079 H HYDROGEN		
	1.0079 H HYDROGEN			10.811 B BORON				
18.998 F FLUORINE			15.999 O OXYGEN		9.0122 Be BERYLLIUM		4.0026 He HELIUM	
		9.0122 Be BERYLLIUM		1.0079 H HYDROGEN		6.941 Li LITHIUM		
	12.011 C CARBON		4.0026 He HELIUM		6.941 Li LITHIUM			18.998 F FLUORINE
				18.998 F FLUORINE			15.999 O OXYGEN	
	15.999 O OXYGEN				12.011 C CARBON			14.007 N NITROGEN
	9.0122 Be BERYLLIUM		6.941 Li LITHIUM					

SWING FOR THE FENCE!

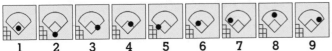
1 2 3 4 5 6 7 8 9

Raine Man
Tim Raines, whose major league career lasted from 1979 to 2002, is the only player in baseball history to steal a base in four separate decades.

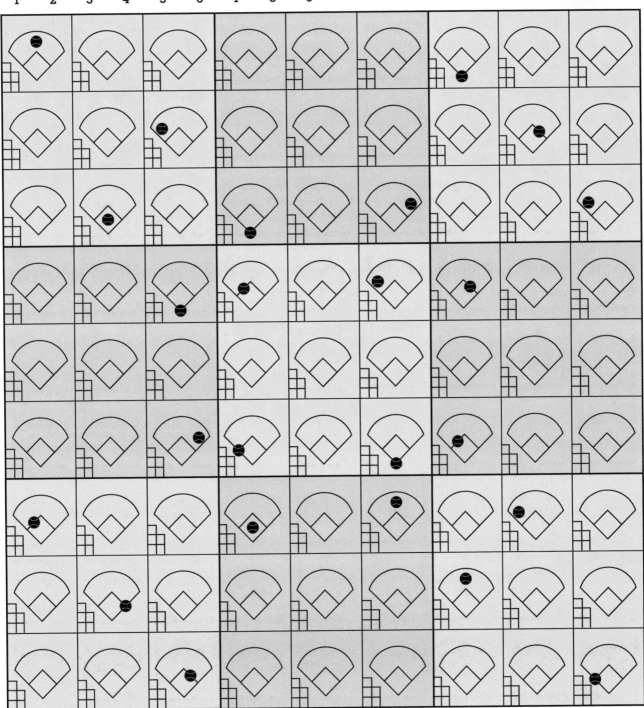

SPEED DIAL

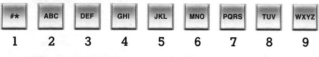

# ✱	ABC	DEF	GHI	JKL	MNO	PQRS	TUV	WXYZ
1	2	3	4	5	6	7	8	9

A Game of Telephone
In Charlie Chaplin's movie *The Circus,* a woman appears to be talking on a cell phone. A clip rediscovered in 2010 caused rumors about time travel, but the device is just an ear trumpet.

PLAYING WITH A FULL DECK

1 2 3 4 5 6 7 8 9

A Poet's Coinage
An early use of the phrase "house of cards" is in John Milton's *Of Reformation Touching Church Discipline* (1641): "to blow them down like a past-bord House built of Court-Cards."

一 二 三 四 五 六 七 八 九
1   2   3   4   5   6   7   8   9

From Worm to Work of Art
Wang Xizhi (307–65), the first great Chinese calligrapher, used silk as the medium for his ink work. It continued to be the medium of choice in China and Japan for seven centuries.

四	二						五	九
六					一			七
					二			
				三		一		
	三	六			七		一	八
				八		五		
					八	四		
五								二
一	七						三	六

SUDO-KUBE

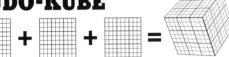

A Steak Out
Cube steak is a thin, tough cut of meat named for the pattern caused by the tenderizing process; it appears to be small cubes, but maintains its shape as a singular slab.

ROCK AROUND THE CLOCK

1   2   3   4   5   6   7   8   9

I'm Late! I'm Late!

In Disney's 1951 animated *Alice in Wonderland*, the Mad Hatter and March Hare attempt to repair the White Rabbit's pocket watch, determining that it is "exactly two days slow."

CARPE SUDOKUM

I	II	III	IV	V	VI	VII	VIII	IX
1	2	3	4	5	6	7	8	9

Eight Days a Week
In A.D. 321, Emperor Constantine, the first Roman emperor to convert to Christianity, officially reduced the week from eight days to seven.

IX							VIII	
		I			VII		V	
	VII		II					I
		VII		IV			IX	
			VIII		V			
	I			IX		VI		
VIII						III		II
	VI		VII				III	
		IX						IV

ALL HAIL BRAILLE

1 2 3 4 5 6 7 8 9

Check It Out
The Library of Congress's National Library Service for the Blind and Physically Handicapped offers over 400,000 free Braille and audio titles through a network of libraries.

204 MEDIUM

GETTING OLD SCHOOLED

⊕ 1 ᲊ 2 Ʊ 3 ⅋ 4 Ꮻ 5 Ꙩ 6 Ӿ 7 ꙍ 8 ꙩꙩ 9

Something Old
The Codex Zographensis, a canon of Old Church Slavonic text discovered in 1843 in the Bulgarian Zograf monastery, was given to Russian Emperor Alexander II as a gift from the monks.

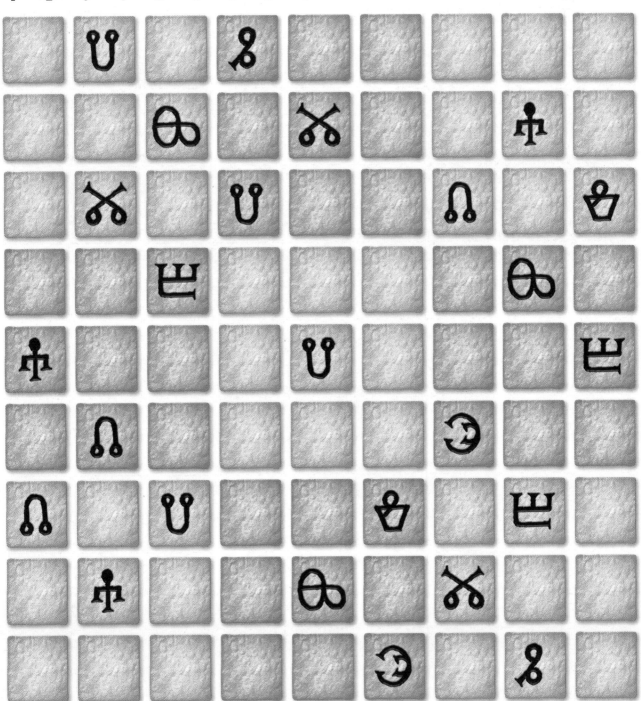

THE DOMINO EFFECT

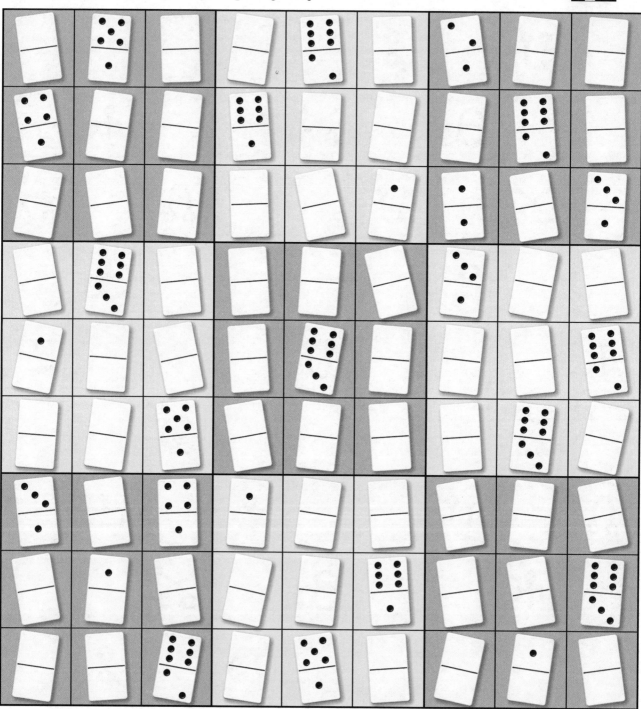

Welcome to Miami, Bienvenido a Miami
Domino Park (aka Máximo Gomez Park) in Miami is *the* gathering place for serious games of dominoes, due in part to the heavy Cuban influence and population.

WHAT'S YOUR SIGN?

1 2 3 4 5 6 7 8 9

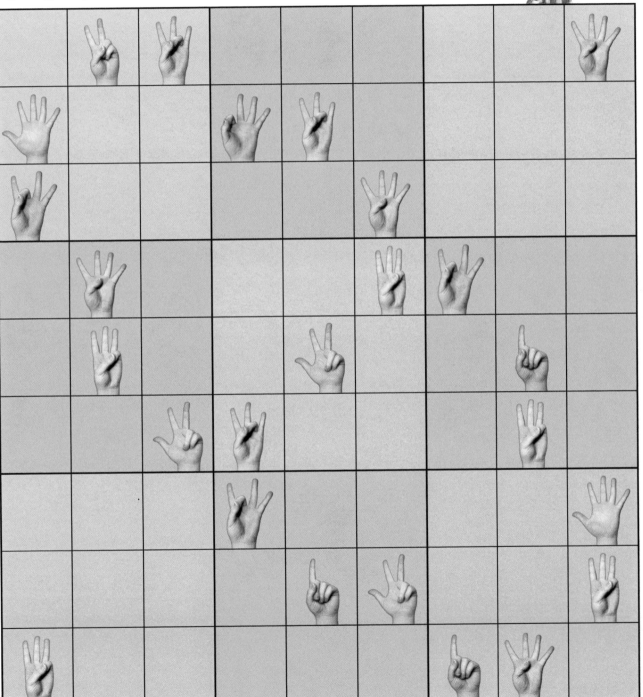

JUST MY TYPE

No More White-Out
IBM introduced early word processing with its 1964 Magnetic Tape/Selectric Typewriter, which had reusable storage that allowed typed material to be edited, saved, and reprinted.

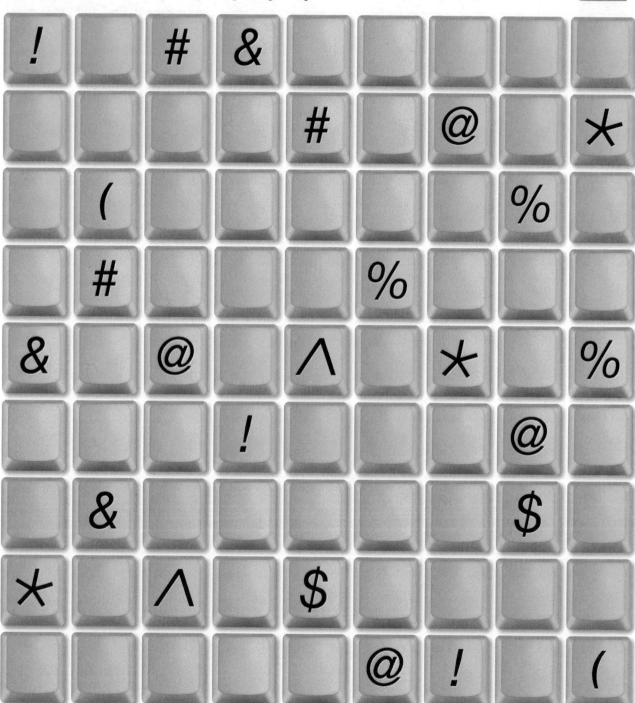

THE ELEMENTS OF STYLE

1	2	3	4	5	6	7	8	9
1.0079 H HYDROGEN	4.0026 He HELIUM	6.941 Li LITHIUM	9.0122 Be BERYLLIUM	10.811 B BORON	12.011 C CARBON	14.007 N NITROGEN	15.999 O OXYGEN	18.998 F FLUORINE

Bodies of Water
It's not just in the air you breathe—oxygen makes up about two-thirds of the human body's mass.

1	2	3	4	5	6	7	8	9
	H					C		Li
Be		He			C			
	Li					B		Be
				H			Be	
			Li		He			
	O			F				
H		N					B	
			H			O		C
F		O					N	

SWING FOR THE FENCE!

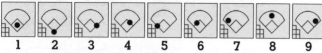

1   2   3   4   5   6   7   8   9

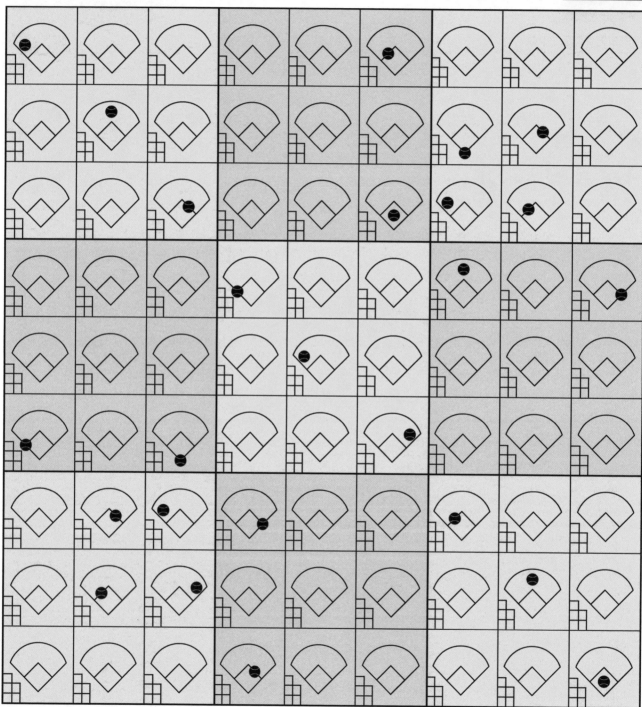

SPEED DIAL

#*	ABC	DEF	GHI	JKL	MNO	PQRS	TUV	WXYZ
1	2	3	4	5	6	7	8	9

Please Leave a Message
The automatic answering machine, created by Willy Muller in 1935, was initially most popular among Orthodox Jews who were forbidden to answer the phone on the Sabbath.

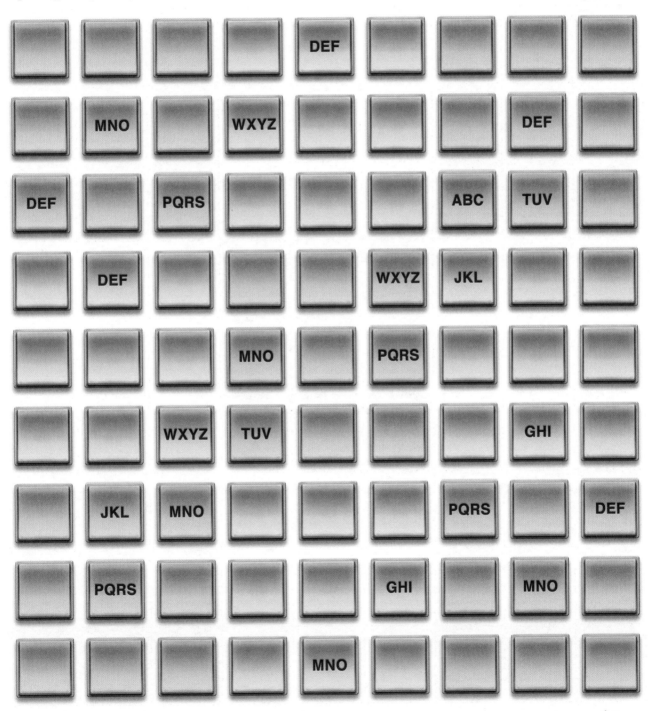

PLAYING WITH A FULL DECK

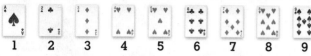

1 2 3 4 5 6 7 8 9

CAST OF CHARACTERS

一	二	三	四	五	六	七	八	九
1	2	3	4	5	6	7	8	9

Calligraphy Inspires Other Arts
In Japan's Edo period (1603–1868), it was fashionable to decorate calligraphy sets with large lacquer scenes, demonstrating the talent of the artist and the affluence of the owner.

三	六	九						
二						九	七	
四							八	
				九	八			
				四	五			
				六	二			
	八							一
	七	二						四
						五	六	三

ROCK AROUND THE CLOCK

Just a Second!
On midnight, January 1, 2008, an extra "leap second" was added to atomic clocks in order to keep their time synced with Earth's rotation.

CARPE SUDOKUM

I	II	III	IV	V	VI	VII	VIII	IX
1	2	3	4	5	6	7	8	9

Super Bowl III
Roman numerals have been used to identify Super Bowl games since 1969, when Lamar Hunt, one of the founders of the NFL, introduced them to bring more stateliness to the game.

		II					V		VII
	V				III				
I				IV					IX
								I	
		IX				III			
	VI								
IX				VII					VI
			V					IV	
VIII		I				II			

ALL HAIL BRAILLE

1 2 3 4 5 6 7 8 9

The Sixth Sense
The best and most beautiful things in the world cannot be seen or even touched. They must be felt within the heart. —**Helen Keller**

GETTING OLD SCHOOLED

Music: The Universal Language
Leoš Janáček's choral and orchestral work *The Glagolitic Mass* was written in Old Church Slavonic, a language that uses the Glagolitic alphabet.

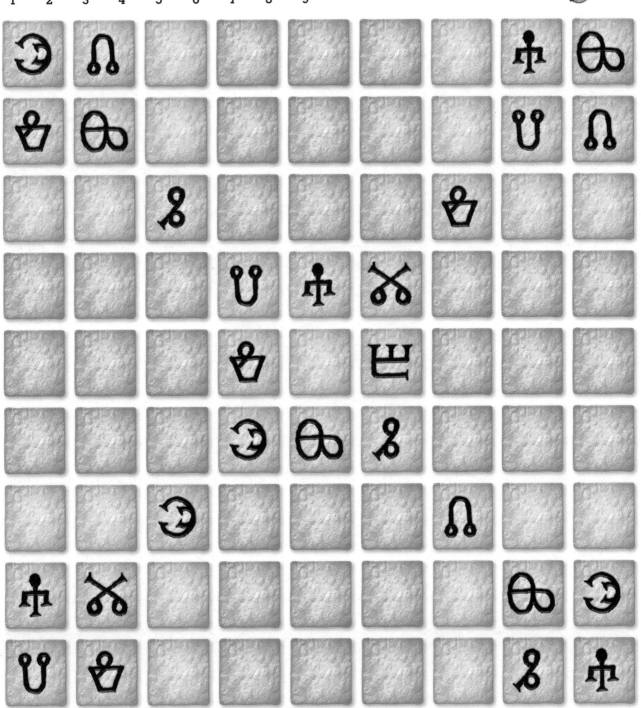

THE DOMINO EFFECT

Dominoes on the Walls
Domino: The Book of Decorating, a portfolio of inspiration based on the former magazine of the same name, is a staple for anyone interested in interior design.

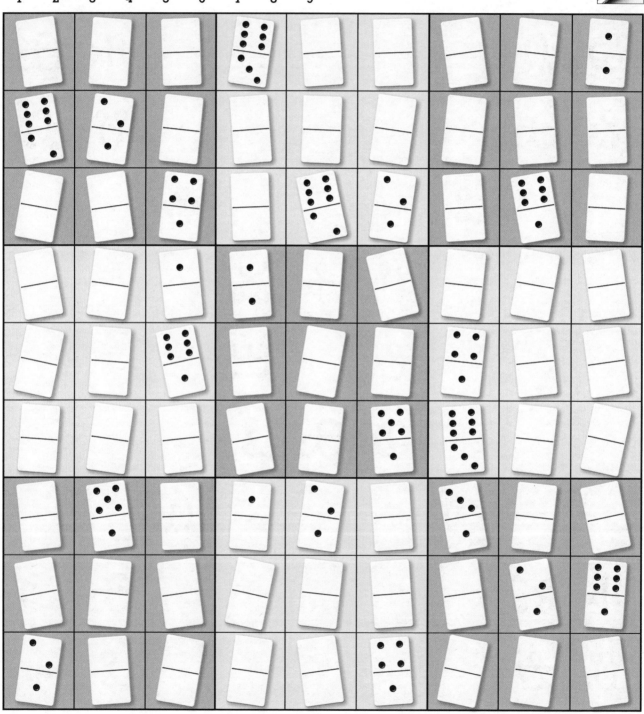

WHAT'S YOUR SIGN?

1 2 3 4 5 6 7 8 9

Silent Heroes
In 1996, two New York City teachers from the School for the Deaf successfully signed down a deaf man threatening to jump off the 22nd floor of a building—from 30 feet away.

JUST MY TYPE

What's Your IM IQ?
Instant messaging (IM) was actually used on multiuser operating systems in the 1960s, well predating the Internet; however, the first IM system with a wide audience launched in 1996.

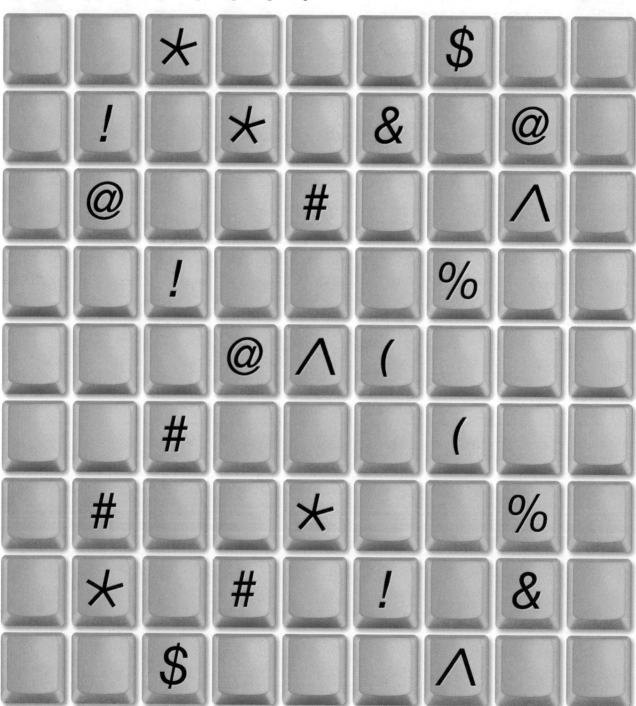

THE ELEMENTS OF STYLE

1.0079 H HYDROGEN	4.0026 He HELIUM	6.941 Li LITHIUM	9.0122 Be BERYLLIUM	10.811 B BORON	12.011 C CARBON	14.007 N NITROGEN	15.999 O OXYGEN	18.998 F FLUORINE
1	2	3	4	5	6	7	8	9

				4.0026 He HELIUM	15.999 O OXYGEN		10.811 B BORON	
		1.0079 H HYDROGEN	10.811 B BORON					9.0122 Be BERYLLIUM
	6.941 Li LITHIUM					18.998 F FLUORINE		
	18.998 F FLUORINE				4.0026 He HELIUM			12.011 C CARBON
10.811 B BORON				6.941 Li LITHIUM				18.998 F FLUORINE
14.007 N NITROGEN			18.998 F FLUORINE				15.999 O OXYGEN	
		4.0026 He HELIUM					18.998 F FLUORINE	
15.999 O OXYGEN					1.0079 H HYDROGEN	12.011 C CARBON		
	1.0079 H HYDROGEN		9.0122 Be BERYLLIUM	12.011 C CARBON				

SWING FOR THE FENCE!

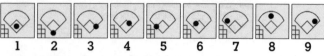

1 2 3 4 5 6 7 8 9

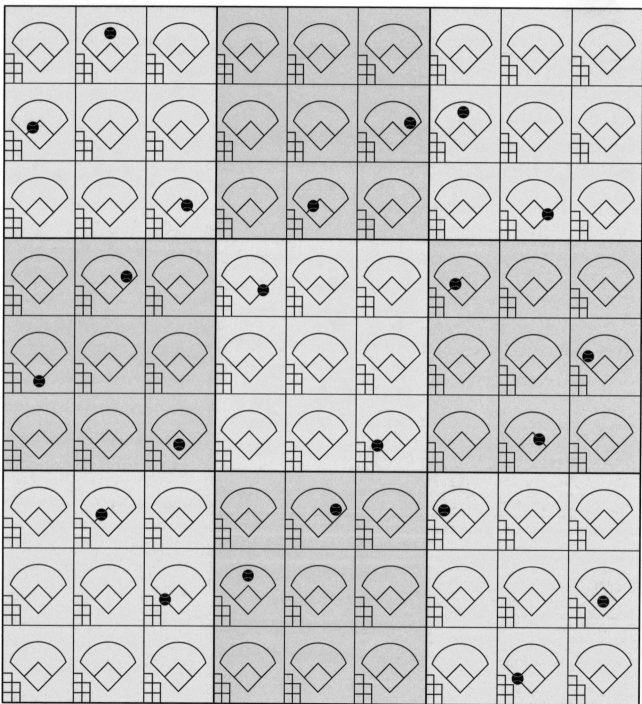

SPEED DIAL

#*	ABC	DEF	GHI	JKL	MNO	PQRS	TUV	WXYZ
1	2	3	4	5	6	7	8	9

La Vie en Rose
The 1954 movie *Sabrina* features a radio mobile car phone that Linus Larrabee (Humphrey Bogart) uses to conduct business on his way to the office.

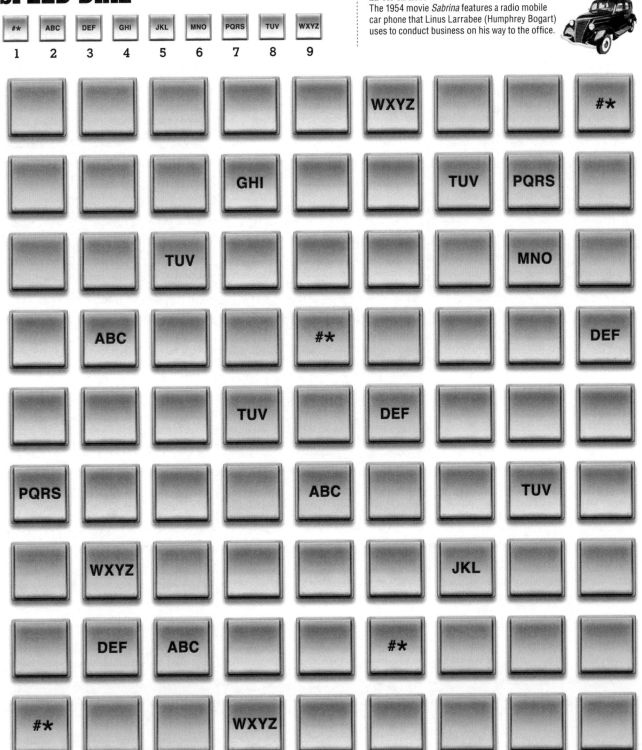

PLAYING WITH A FULL DECK

Deck Someone
Cards are war, in disguise of a sport.
—Charles Lamb

CAST OF CHARACTERS

一	二	三	四	五	六	七	八	九
1	2	3	4	5	6	7	8	9

Them Bones
"Oracle-bone script"—a form that appeared on bones used for divination in China from the second millennium B.C.—is said to be the beginning of Chinese painting and calligraphy.

	四	六		三	八			
	九	三		四	一			
	七	五						
	三	四				七	八	
						九	二	
			五	九		八	七	
			四	七		三	六	

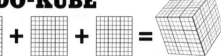

ROCK AROUND THE CLOCK

1 2 3 4 5 6 7 8 9

CARPE SUDOKUM

When in Rome . . .
Though the origins of this phrase (first written in Latin) date back as early as A.D. 390, the earliest known appearance of the proverb in English was recorded in a 1777 publication.

I	II	III	IV	V	VI	VII	VIII	IX
1	2	3	4	5	6	7	8	9

	VIII							
							VIII	VI
IX		VII			VIII	V	IV	
		V			I	VIII		
			III		IV			
		I	IX			IV		
	III	IX	I			VII		II
II	I							
							III	

ALL HAIL BRAILLE

1　2　3　4　5　6　7　8　9

Speed Reading
Because Braille is larger than print, words can be shortened into "contractions." In Grade 2 Braille, students learn to read contractions, in which one letter can stand for a whole word.

GETTING OLD SCHOOLED

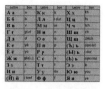

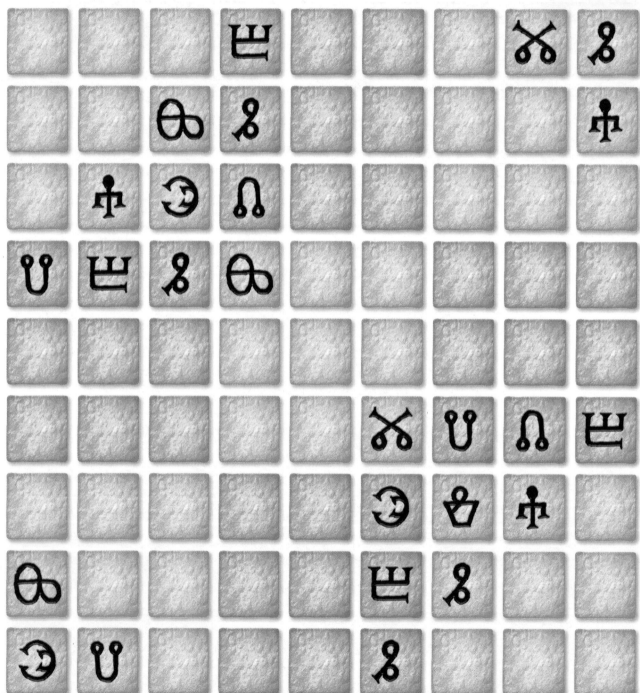

THE DOMINO EFFECT

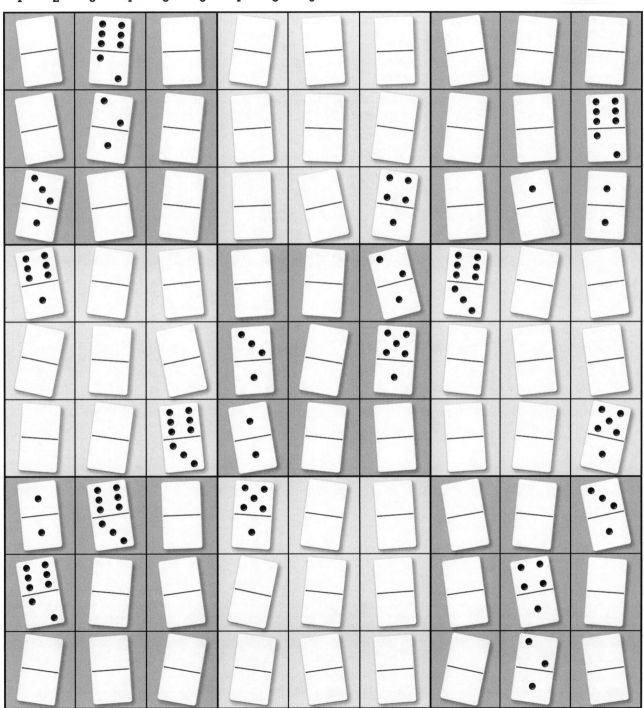

Hit "Play"
Domino Recording Company, an independent British record label, was responsible for the success of hit bands Franz Ferdinand and the Arctic Monkeys.

1 2 3 4 5 6 7 8 9

Signing "Woof!"
Who says you can't teach a deaf dog new tricks? Hogan, a deaf Dalmatian, knows up to 65 words in sign language.

				7				
	4						7	
				7	2	5		
		7					4	
4		4					5	2
		5					3	
			3	5	7			
	7						1	
				4				

JUST MY TYPE

!	@	#	$	%	∧	&	*	(
1	2	3	4	5	6	7	8	9

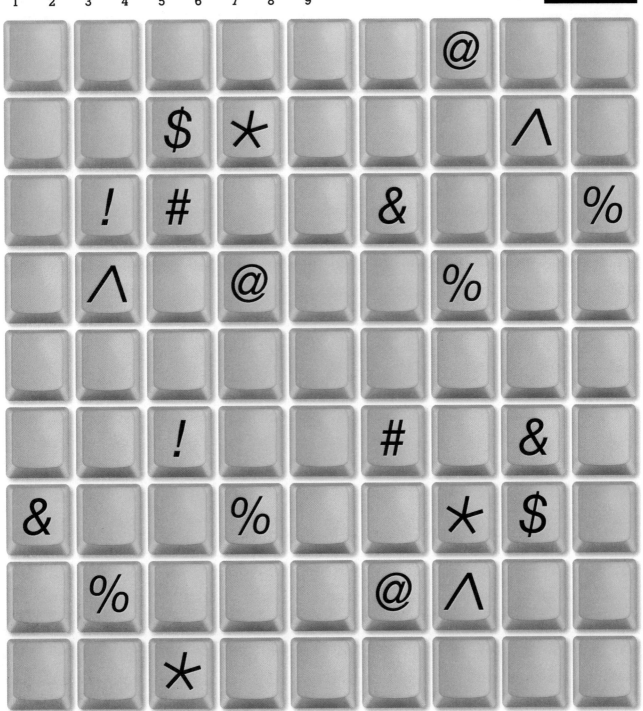

THE ELEMENTS OF STYLE

1.0079	4.0026	6.941	9.0122	10.811	12.011	14.007	15.999	18.998
H	He	Li	Be	B	C	N	O	F
HYDROGEN	HELIUM	LITHIUM	BERYLLIUM	BORON	CARBON	NITROGEN	OXYGEN	FLUORINE
1	2	3	4	5	6	7	8	9

The Gold Rush
Nobel Laureate Glenn T. Seaborg successfully transmuted lead into gold in 1951, achieving what medieval alchemists could not; he also created the element plutonium.

C (12.011)					N (14.007)		B (10.811)	
			Be (9.0122)	Li (6.941)				
		He (4.0026)				O (15.999)		F (18.998)
	Li (6.941)				Be (9.0122)			
O (15.999)		C (12.011)				H (1.0079)		He (4.0026)
			H (1.0079)				O (15.999)	
Be (9.0122)		Li (6.941)				C (12.011)		
				He (4.0026)	B (10.811)			
	B (10.811)		N (14.007)					H (1.0079)

SWING FOR THE FENCE!

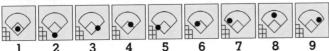

1 2 3 4 5 6 7 8 9

Night Game
On May 16, 1939, Shibe Park in Philadelphia was home to the first American League game that wasn't played during the middle of the day.

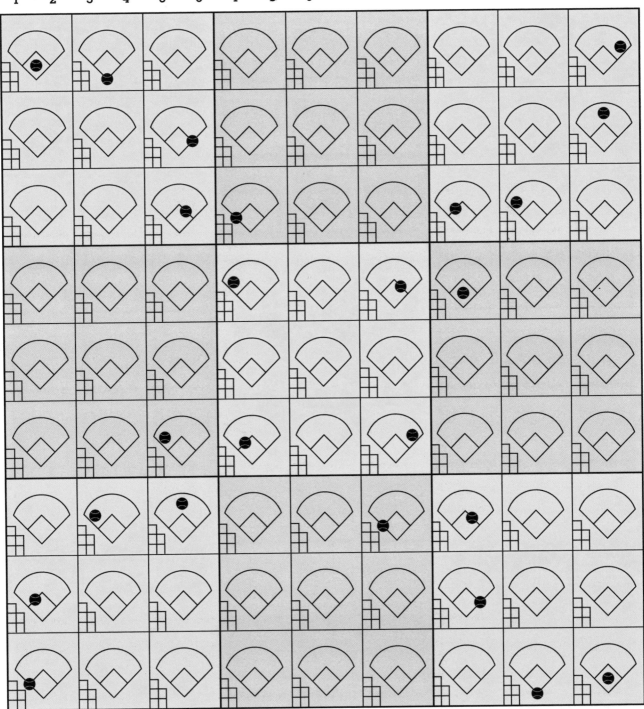

SPEED DIAL

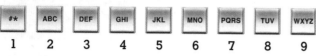

1	2	3	4	5	6	7	8	9
#*	ABC	DEF	GHI	JKL	MNO	PQRS	TUV	WXYZ

Three Nines Means Help

In 1937, Great Britain implemented the first emergency phone system, through which the country's residents could seek help by dialing 999. The United States soon adopted a similar system.

PLAYING WITH A FULL DECK

CAST OF CHARACTERS

一 二 三 四 五 六 七 八 九
1　2　3　4　5　6　7　8　9

Pick up Sticks
Ink for Japanese calligraphy is usually sold in solidified form, or in ink "sticks." The sticks are made from wood and vegetable oils that are burned into soot.

	五						二	
六								一
			八	九		三	六	
			五		四		七	
				六	七	二		
				四	三		九	
			三	四		一	五	
四								七
	一						三	

ROCK AROUND THE CLOCK

1 2 3 4 5 6 7 8 9

The Science Behind the Bling
Rolex has over 1,000 patents in horology, the science of measuring time. One such patent covers the self-winding movement of its watches.

CARPE SUDOKUM

I	II	III	IV	V	VI	VII	VIII	IX
1	2	3	4	5	6	7	8	9

Tick Tock
Clock faces with Roman numerals often use IIII, rather than IV, to visually balance out the VIII on the other side of the face.

	III				VI	IX		
VII							I	
		II	VIII				III	
		I	V					III
V								VI
IV					III	II		
	IX				I	IV		
		V						VIII
			VII	III			VI	

240 ⌂HARD

ALL HAIL BRAILLE

⠁	⠃	⠉	⠙	⠑	⠋	⠛	⠓	⠊
1	2	3	4	5	6	7	8	9

Follow the Leader
Typically, Braille is read with the first finger of both hands: The right hand reads first, while the left is used to confirm and to drop down to the next line of cells for a smooth transition.

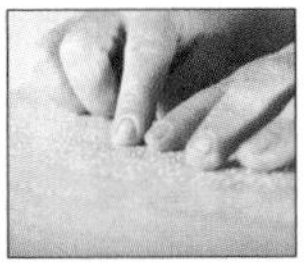

							⠓	
	⠉		⠃				⠑	⠋
		⠊			⠁	⠛		
	⠃		⠋			⠁		
				⠉				
		⠉			⠊		⠙	
		⠃	⠉			⠙		
⠙	⠁				⠛		⠊	
	⠛							

GETTING OLD SCHOOLED

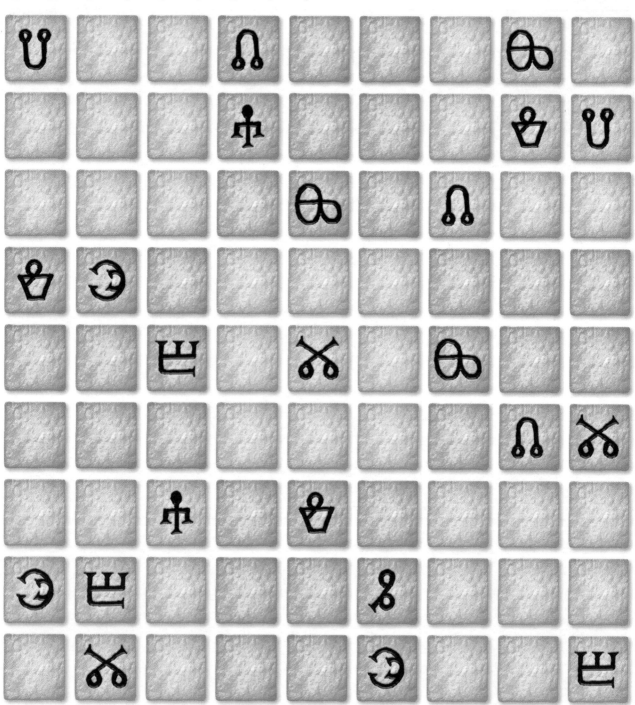

THE DOMINO EFFECT

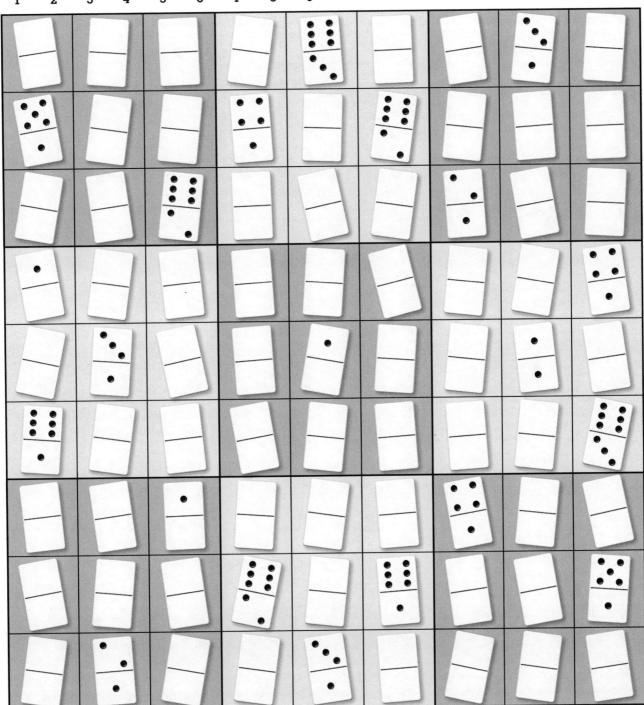

A Domino Duel
In 1873, Confederate Col. Henry Theodore Titus defeated Capt. Clark Rice in a domino match to determine who would name the beach town of Sand Point, now Titusville, Florida.

WHAT'S YOUR SIGN?

1 2 3 4 5 6 7 8 9

JUST MY TYPE

!	@	#	$	%	∧	&	*	(
1	2	3	4	5	6	7	8	9

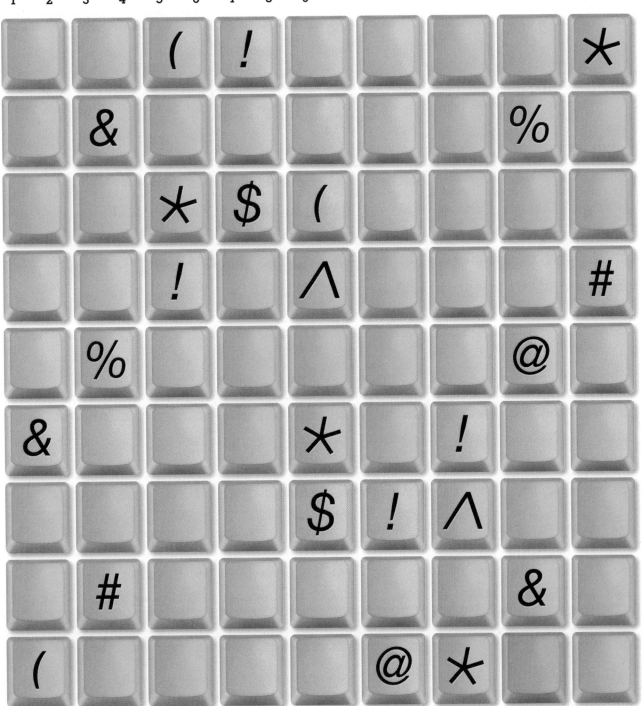

THE ELEMENTS OF STYLE

1.0079 H HYDROGEN	4.0026 He HELIUM	6.941 Li LITHIUM	9.0122 Be BERYLLIUM	10.811 B BORON	12.011 C CARBON	14.007 N NITROGEN	15.999 O OXYGEN	18.998 F FLUORINE
1	2	3	4	5	6	7	8	9

USA, USA!
A very small amount of americium-241, the only synthetic element to have made its way into regular household use, is the main component of smoke detectors.

			10.811 B BORON		4.0026 He HELIUM			
	9.0122 Be BERYLLIUM			6.941 Li LITHIUM			10.811 B BORON	
		6.941 Li LITHIUM				15.999 O OXYGEN		
12.011 C CARBON			1.0079 H HYDROGEN		15.999 O OXYGEN			10.811 B BORON
	15.999 O OXYGEN						14.007 N NITROGEN	
18.998 F FLUORINE			4.0026 He HELIUM		12.011 C CARBON			1.0079 H HYDROGEN
		14.007 N NITROGEN				4.0026 He HELIUM		
	12.011 C CARBON			9.0122 Be BERYLLIUM			6.941 Li LITHIUM	
			15.999 O OXYGEN		18.998 F FLUORINE			

SWING FOR THE FENCE!

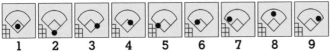

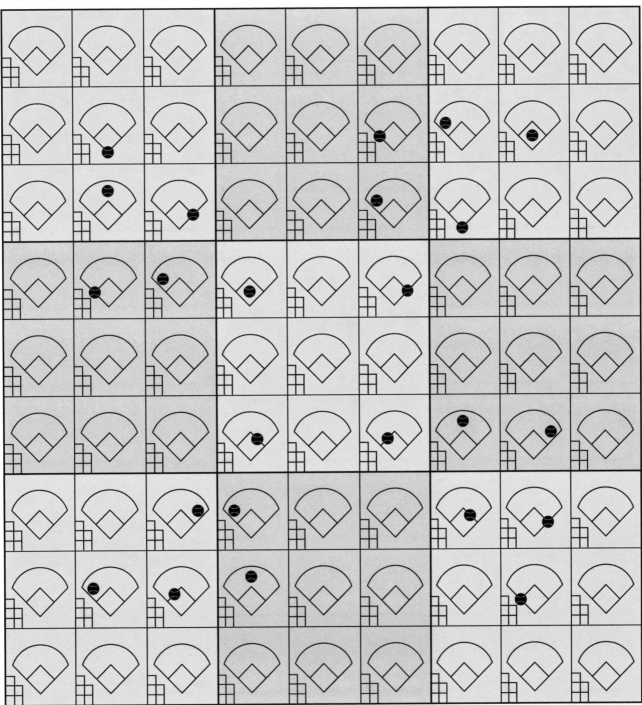

SPEED DIAL

#*	ABC	DEF	GHI	JKL	MNO	PQRS	TUV	WXYZ
1	2	3	4	5	6	7	8	9

Rikki Don't Lose that Number!
In his 2008 hit single "Kiss Me Thru the Phone," hip-hop artist Soulja Boy includes the number (678) 999-8212. Fans who called the number got a recorded message from Soulja Boy.

#*				PQRS				DEF
	ABC					MNO		
		DEF				#*	WXYZ	
			GHI			ABC		
MNO				JKL				TUV
		TUV			MNO			
	GHI		MNO			PQRS		
		ABC					TUV	
TUV				DEF				WXYZ

PLAYING WITH A FULL DECK

Easier Than You Think

The probability of drawing an ace from a random deck of 52 cards in a single draw is one out of 13.

CAST OF CHARACTERS

一 二 三 四 五 六 七 八 九
1　2　3　4　5　6　7　8　9

					三	五		
					九	六		
		九	四					二
		八	二					
二								一
五					六	四		八
四					七	三		
		七	五					
		六	一					

SUDO-KUBE

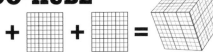

The Rubik's Run
Uli Kilian set a world record when he solved 100 Rubik's Cubes while running the London Marathon in 4 hours and 45 minutes (that's one puzzle every three minutes).

ROCK AROUND THE CLOCK

1 2 3 4 5 6 7 8 9

A Royal Minute
In 1675, Charles II founded the Royal Observatory in Greenwich, England, the home of Greenwich Mean Time and the Prime Meridian.

CARPE SUDOKUM

What's in a Name?
Roman Emperor Numerian, or Marcus Aurelius Numerius Numerianus, ruled Rome with his brother Carinus for about one year, from A.D. 283 to 284.

I	II	III	IV	V	VI	VII	VIII	IX
1	2	3	4	5	6	7	8	9

VIII								V
				IX	IV			
		IX		I		II		
			VII		IV		III	
	III	II				V	VIII	
	I		VIII		III			
		VIII		VII		IX		
				III	II			
V								VI

Textured Tattoos
Klara Jirkova, a student at the University of the Arts Berlin, brainstormed a surgical steel implant that could be inserted under the skin to make a series of raised dots—a Braille tattoo.

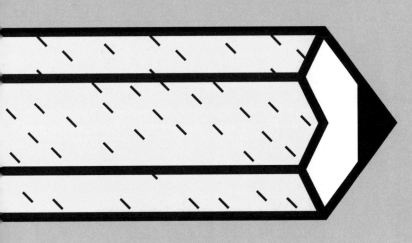

SOLUTIONS

P. 2

P. 3

III	IV	VII	V	IX	II	VIII	I	VI
IX	V	VI	VII	I	VIII	III	IV	II
I	VIII	II	VI	III	IV	VII	V	IX
II	IX	IV	I	V	III	VI	VIII	VII
V	VII	I	VIII	VI	IX	II	III	IV
VIII	VI	III	II	IV	VII	V	IX	I
VII	I	IX	III	II	V	IV	VI	VIII
IV	II	V	IX	VIII	VI	I	VII	III
VI	III	VIII	IV	VII	I	IX	II	V

P. 4

P. 5

P. 6

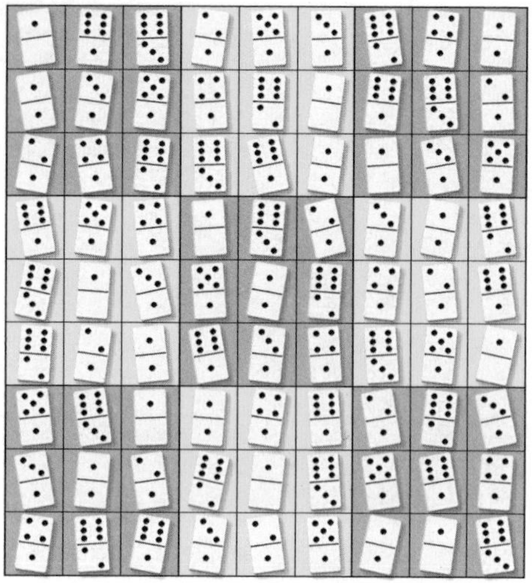

P. 7

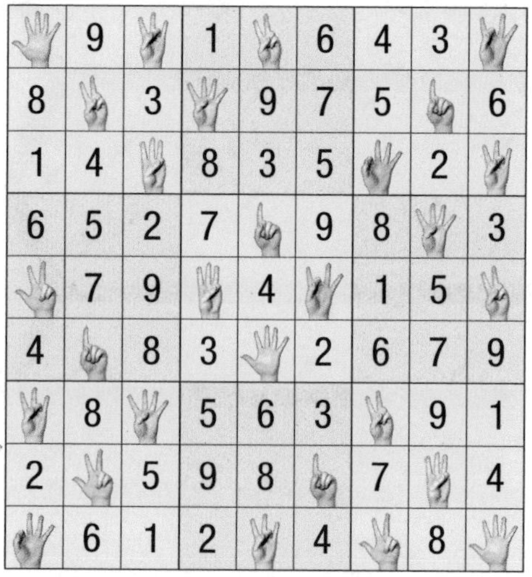

P. 8

#	*	(	&	$	%	!	^	@
@	$	%	!	^	#	*	&	(
^	!	&	(	@	*	$	#	%
%	&	#	^	*	@	(	$	!
$	(	^	%	!	&	#	@	*
!	@	*	#	(	$	&	%	^
(	#	$	*	%	^	@	!	&
&	%	!	@	#	(	^	*	$
*	^	@	$	&	!	%	(	#

P. 9

15.999 O OXYGEN	18.998 F FLUORINE	14.007 N NITROGEN	4.0026 He HELIUM	1.0079 H HYDROGEN	12.011 C CARBON	9.0122 Be BERYLLIUM	6.941 Li LITHIUM	10.811 B BORON
12.011 C CARBON	4.0026 He HELIUM	1.0079 H HYDROGEN	10.811 B BORON	6.941 Li LITHIUM	9.0122 Be BERYLLIUM	14.007 N NITROGEN	15.999 O OXYGEN	18.998 F FLUORINE
6.941 Li LITHIUM	9.0122 Be BERYLLIUM	10.811 B BORON	18.998 F FLUORINE	14.007 N NITROGEN	15.999 O OXYGEN	4.0026 He HELIUM	12.011 C CARBON	1.0079 H HYDROGEN
9.0122 Be BERYLLIUM	6.941 Li LITHIUM	12.011 C CARBON	14.007 N NITROGEN	15.999 O OXYGEN	18.998 F FLUORINE	10.811 B BORON	1.0079 H HYDROGEN	4.0026 He HELIUM
14.007 N NITROGEN	10.811 B BORON	18.998 F FLUORINE	6.941 Li LITHIUM	4.0026 He HELIUM	1.0079 H HYDROGEN	15.999 O OXYGEN	9.0122 Be BERYLLIUM	12.011 C CARBON
1.0079 H HYDROGEN	15.999 O OXYGEN	4.0026 He HELIUM	12.011 C CARBON	9.0122 Be BERYLLIUM	10.811 B BORON	6.941 Li LITHIUM	18.998 F FLUORINE	14.007 N NITROGEN
4.0026 He HELIUM	14.007 N NITROGEN	9.0122 Be BERYLLIUM	1.0079 H HYDROGEN	12.011 C CARBON	6.941 Li LITHIUM	18.998 F FLUORINE	10.811 B BORON	15.999 O OXYGEN
10.811 B BORON	1.0079 H HYDROGEN	6.941 Li LITHIUM	15.999 O OXYGEN	18.998 F FLUORINE	14.007 N NITROGEN	12.011 C CARBON	4.0026 He HELIUM	9.0122 Be BERYLLIUM
18.998 F FLUORINE	12.011 C CARBON	15.999 O OXYGEN	9.0122 Be BERYLLIUM	10.811 B BORON	4.0026 He HELIUM	1.0079 H HYDROGEN	14.007 N NITROGEN	6.941 Li LITHIUM

P. 10

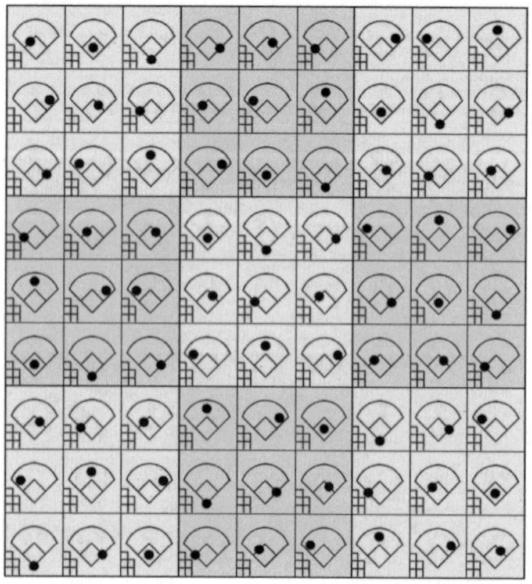

P. 11

WXYZ	DEF	PQRS	TUV	ABC	GHI	MNO	#*	JKL
ABC	MNO	TUV	WXYZ	JKL	#*	PQRS	DEF	GHI
#*	JKL	GHI	DEF	MNO	PQRS	ABC	TUV	WXYZ
JKL	#*	WXYZ	GHI	TUV	ABC	DEF	PQRS	MNO
TUV	PQRS	ABC	JKL	DEF	MNO	WXYZ	GHI	#*
DEF	GHI	MNO	#*	PQRS	WXYZ	TUV	JKL	ABC
PQRS	WXYZ	JKL	MNO	#*	TUV	GHI	ABC	DEF
MNO	TUV	#*	ABC	GHI	DEF	JKL	WXYZ	PQRS
GHI	ABC	DEF	PQRS	WXYZ	JKL	#*	MNO	TUV

P. 12

8		3	5		9	2		6
9	6		3	1		8	4	
	7	2		4	8		5	9
	9	7		6	5		8	3
5		6	9		1	7		4
4	8			3		9	6	
6	1		7	9		5	3	
	5	9		2	6		7	8
7		4	8		3	6		1

P. 13

五	一	八	九	二	六	七	四	三
四	二	九	七	三	八	六	一	五
三	七	六	四	一	五	八	二	九
八	五	三	二	六	一	四	九	七
七	九	一	三	八	四	五	六	二
六	四	二	五	九	七	一	三	八
一	三	五	六	七	二	九	八	四
九	八	四	一	五	三	二	七	六
二	六	七	八	四	九	三	五	一

P. 14

P. 15

I	IV	VI	VII	III	V	IX	VIII	II
II	VII	V	IX	I	VIII	III	IV	VI
VIII	IX	III	II	VI	IV	I	V	VII
VII	V	IX	III	VIII	I	VI	II	IV
IV	III	II	V	IX	VI	VIII	VII	I
VI	VIII	I	IV	VII	II	V	IX	III
IX	I	IV	VI	V	VII	II	III	VIII
V	VI	VII	VIII	II	III	IV	I	IX
III	II	VIII	I	IV	IX	VII	VI	V

P. 16

P. 17

P. 18

P. 19

P. 20

!	★	(	$	&	@	#	%	∧
∧	#	$	!	★	%	@	&	(
%	&	@	#	∧	(	$	★	!
#	∧	!	&	%	★	(	$	@
&	@	★	(	$	∧	%	!	#
$	(	%	@	#	!	&	∧	★
(	!	&	★	@	$	∧	#	%
★	%	#	∧	(	&	!	@	$
@	$	∧	%	!	#	★	(	&

P. 21

Li	C	F	B	He	N	H	Be	O
H	B	He	F	O	Be	N	C	Li
N	Be	O	H	Li	C	B	F	He
He	F	Li	O	C	H	Be	B	N
B	O	H	Be	N	Li	F	He	C
Be	N	C	He	F	B	Li	O	H
C	Li	B	N	Be	He	O	H	F
O	H	N	C	B	F	He	Li	Be
F	He	Be	Li	H	O	C	N	B

P. 22

P. 23

ABC	PQRS	JKL	DEF	MNO	TUV	#★	GHI	WXYZ
GHI	#★	MNO	PQRS	JKL	WXYZ	TUV	DEF	ABC
TUV	DEF	WXYZ	ABC	#★	GHI	JKL	PQRS	MNO
#★	GHI	PQRS	MNO	TUV	ABC	DEF	WXYZ	JKL
MNO	WXYZ	ABC	JKL	GHI	DEF	PQRS	TUV	#★
DEF	JKL	TUV	#★	WXYZ	PQRS	ABC	MNO	GHI
PQRS	MNO	#★	WXYZ	DEF	JKL	GHI	ABC	TUV
JKL	TUV	DEF	GHI	ABC	MNO	WXYZ	#★	PQRS
WXYZ	ABC	GHI	TUV	PQRS	#★	MNO	JKL	DEF

P. 24

8	2	1	♦	6	4	3	♥	♥
7	4	♣	8	♦	9	6	1	♠
9	♦	6	5	2	♠	7	8	4
♥	6	3	♣	4	7	♥	9	1
4	♥	8	1	♣	3	2	♦	6
1	7	♣	9	8	♣	4	3	♠
3	5	7	♠	1	2	9	♣	8
♣	8	4	3	♥	5	♠	2	7
♥	♠	9	6	7	♣	5	4	3

P. 25

六九三二七四五八一
五八七九一六三四二
二一四八五三九七六
四三五六二九八一七
七二九四八一六三五
八六一七三五二九四
九四二一六八七五三
一五六三九七四二八
三七八五四二一六九

P. 26

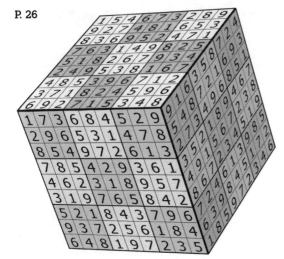

P. 27

(clock-face solution grid)

P. 28

V	II	IX	IV	I	III	VII	VI	VIII
VIII	I	VI	VII	II	IX	V	III	IV
VII	III	IV	VI	V	VIII	II	IX	I
VI	IV	III	V	IX	I	VIII	VII	II
II	V	VII	VIII	VI	IV	III	I	IX
I	IX	VIII	II	III	VII	IV	V	VI
IV	VIII	V	IX	VII	VI	I	II	III
IX	VII	I	III	IV	II	VI	VIII	V
III	VI	II	I	VIII	V	IX	IV	VII

P. 29

(braille-dot solution grid)

P. 30

P. 31

P. 32

P. 33

P. 34

12.011	14.007	4.0026	1.0079	10.811	9.0122	18.998	6.941	15.999
C	N	He	H	B	Be	F	Li	O
CARBON	NITROGEN	HELIUM	HYDROGEN	BORON	BERYLLIUM	FLUORINE	LITHIUM	OXYGEN
15.999	10.811	18.998	6.941	4.0026	14.007	1.0079	12.011	9.0122
O	B	F	Li	He	N	H	C	Be
OXYGEN	BORON	FLUORINE	LITHIUM	HELIUM	NITROGEN	HYDROGEN	CARBON	BERYLLIUM
6.941	1.0079	9.0122	12.011	15.999	18.998	10.811	4.0026	14.007
Li	H	Be	C	O	F	B	He	N
LITHIUM	HYDROGEN	BERYLLIUM	CARBON	OXYGEN	FLUORINE	BORON	HELIUM	NITROGEN
10.811	6.941	14.007	15.999	12.011	4.0026	9.0122	18.998	1.0079
B	Li	N	O	C	He	Be	F	H
BORON	LITHIUM	NITROGEN	OXYGEN	CARBON	HELIUM	BERYLLIUM	FLUORINE	HYDROGEN
9.0122	12.011	15.999	18.998	6.941	1.0079	14.007	10.811	4.0026
Be	C	O	F	Li	H	N	B	He
BERYLLIUM	CARBON	OXYGEN	FLUORINE	LITHIUM	HYDROGEN	NITROGEN	BORON	HELIUM
18.998	4.0026	1.0079	14.007	9.0122	10.811	6.941	15.999	12.011
F	He	H	N	Be	B	Li	O	C
FLUORINE	HELIUM	HYDROGEN	NITROGEN	BERYLLIUM	BORON	LITHIUM	OXYGEN	CARBON
14.007	9.0122	12.011	4.0026	18.998	6.941	15.999	1.0079	10.811
N	Be	C	He	F	Li	O	H	B
NITROGEN	BERYLLIUM	CARBON	HELIUM	FLUORINE	LITHIUM	OXYGEN	HYDROGEN	BORON
1.0079	15.999	6.941	10.811	14.007	12.011	4.0026	9.0122	18.998
H	O	Li	B	N	C	He	Be	F
HYDROGEN	OXYGEN	LITHIUM	BORON	NITROGEN	CARBON	HELIUM	BERYLLIUM	FLUORINE
4.0026	18.999	10.811	9.0122	1.0079	15.999	12.011	14.007	6.941
He	F	B	Be	H	O	C	N	Li
HELIUM	FLUORINE	BORON	BERYLLIUM	HYDROGEN	OXYGEN	CARBON	NITROGEN	LITHIUM

P. 35

P. 36

TUV	WXYZ	MNO	ABC	GHI	JKL	#★	DEF	PQRS
JKL	ABC	DEF	PQRS	WXYZ	#★	TUV	MNO	GHI
#★	PQRS	GHI	TUV	DEF	MNO	ABC	WXYZ	JKL
WXYZ	TUV	JKL	DEF	#★	PQRS	GHI	ABC	MNO
MNO	DEF	ABC	GHI	JKL	TUV	WXYZ	PQRS	#★
GHI	#★	PQRS	WXYZ	MNO	ABC	JKL	TUV	DEF
PQRS	GHI	TUV	#★	ABC	DEF	MNO	JKL	WXYZ
ABC	MNO	#★	JKL	PQRS	WXYZ	DEF	GHI	TUV
DEF	JKL	WXYZ	MNO	TUV	GHI	PQRS	#★	ABC

P. 37

1	🂡	🃁	7	2	🂱	4	3	🃑
🂾	3	8	♠	6	5	🂹	🃉	2
7	5	2	9	3	4	6	8	1
3	4	5	6	8	1	🃂	🂢	9
🂪	6	7	🂺	4	🂧	8	1	🃃
8	♠	🂻	3	7	2	5	4	6
6	2	1	8	5	7	3	9	4
9	🃇	🃗	4	1	🂥	2	5	🂲
🂴	8	4	🃄	9	3	♠	🃖	7

P. 38

七	三	六	四	九	五	二	八	一
五	八	二	三	七	一	九	六	四
一	九	四	八	二	六	七	五	三
八	一	七	二	三	九	六	四	五
二	五	九	六	一	四	三	七	八
六	四	三	七	五	八	一	二	九
三	六	一	五	四	七	八	九	二
四	二	八	九	六	三	五	一	七
九	七	五	一	八	二	四	三	六

P. 39

P. 40

IV	VII	II	I	III	V	VIII	IX	VI
V	IX	VI	II	VIII	VII	III	I	IV
III	I	VIII	IV	VI	IX	II	V	VII
VIII	V	I	IX	IV	VI	VII	III	II
VII	III	IX	VIII	I	II	VI	IV	V
II	VI	IV	VII	V	III	IX	VIII	I
IX	VIII	VII	V	II	I	IV	VI	III
I	II	III	VI	IX	IV	V	VII	VIII
VI	IV	V	III	VII	VIII	I	II	IX

P. 41

261

SOLUTIONS

P. 42

P. 43

P. 44

		3	8	1	6	7		
	8	2	9		7	3	1	
1	7	4		2		6	8	9
8	4		2		3		6	1
9		1		5		8		3
3	6		7		1		9	2
7	5	6		3		2	4	8
	3	9	4		8	1	5	
		8	5	7	2	9		

P. 45

@	%	#	!	∧	(	&	$	⋆
(	∧	&	$	⋆	@	!	%	#
⋆	!	$	#	%	&	(	∧	@
!	⋆	%	∧	@	$	#	(	&
$	#	@	&	(	%	∧	⋆	!
&	(	∧	⋆	#	!	$	@	%
∧	&	!	@	$	⋆	%	#	(
#	@	(	%	&	∧	⋆	!	$
%	$	⋆	(	!	#	@	&	∧

P. 46

14.007 N NITROGEN	6.941 Li LITHIUM	12.011 C CARBON	15.999 O OXYGEN	9.0122 Be BERYLLIUM	1.0079 H HYDROGEN	10.811 B BORON	18.998 F FLUORINE	4.0026 He HELIUM
10.811 B BORON	1.0079 H HYDROGEN	9.0122 Be BERYLLIUM	4.0026 He HELIUM	18.998 F FLUORINE	6.941 Li LITHIUM	15.999 O OXYGEN	12.011 C CARBON	14.007 N NITROGEN
4.0026 He HELIUM	15.999 O OXYGEN	18.998 F FLUORINE	12.011 C CARBON	14.007 N NITROGEN	10.811 B BORON	1.0079 H HYDROGEN	9.0122 Be BERYLLIUM	6.941 Li LITHIUM
15.999 O OXYGEN	14.007 N NITROGEN	1.0079 H HYDROGEN	10.811 B BORON	6.941 Li LITHIUM	18.998 F FLUORINE	12.011 C CARBON	4.0026 He HELIUM	9.0122 Be BERYLLIUM
9.0122 Be BERYLLIUM	4.0026 He HELIUM	10.811 B BORON	14.007 N NITROGEN	15.999 O OXYGEN	12.011 C CARBON	6.941 Li LITHIUM	1.0079 H HYDROGEN	18.998 F FLUORINE
18.998 F FLUORINE	12.011 C CARBON	6.941 Li LITHIUM	1.0079 H HYDROGEN	4.0026 He HELIUM	9.0122 Be BERYLLIUM	14.007 N NITROGEN	10.811 B BORON	15.999 O OXYGEN
6.941 Li LITHIUM	10.811 B BORON	15.999 O OXYGEN	18.998 F FLUORINE	12.011 C CARBON	4.0026 He HELIUM	9.0122 Be BERYLLIUM	14.007 N NITROGEN	1.0079 H HYDROGEN
12.011 C CARBON	18.998 F FLUORINE	14.007 N NITROGEN	9.0122 Be BERYLLIUM	1.0079 H HYDROGEN	15.999 O OXYGEN	4.0026 He HELIUM	6.941 Li LITHIUM	10.811 B BORON
1.0079 H HYDROGEN	9.0122 Be BERYLLIUM	4.0026 He HELIUM	6.941 Li LITHIUM	10.811 B BORON	14.007 N NITROGEN	18.998 F FLUORINE	15.999 O OXYGEN	12.011 C CARBON

P. 47

P. 48

GHI	ABC	#★	TUV	WXYZ	MNO	JKL	DEF	PQRS
JKL	MNO	PQRS	DEF	ABC	GHI	#★	WXYZ	TUV
WXYZ	TUV	DEF	PQRS	JKL	#★	MNO	GHI	ABC
DEF	#★	MNO	GHI	TUV	WXYZ	ABC	PQRS	JKL
TUV	PQRS	WXYZ	JKL	#★	ABC	DEF	MNO	GHI
ABC	GHI	JKL	MNO	DEF	PQRS	TUV	#★	WXYZ
PQRS	JKL	GHI	ABC	MNO	DEF	WXYZ	TUV	#★
MNO	WXYZ	ABC	#★	GHI	TUV	PQRS	JKL	DEF
#★	DEF	TUV	WXYZ	PQRS	JKL	GHI	ABC	MNO

P. 49

♥	8	2	♣	3	♦	5	6	♠
♣	7	3	1	♠	4	8	9	♥
1	♦	5	2	8	6	4	♣	3
8	4	♥	5	1	2	♣	3	6
5	1	9	♦	♣	♥	2	4	7
2	3	♣	9	4	7	♠	8	5
7	♥	8	4	2	3	6	♠	9
♦	6	1	8	♣	5	3	2	♥
♠	2	4	♣	9	♠	7	♥	8

P. 50

八	一	三	七	九	五	四	二	六
二	五	九	三	六	四	八	一	七
四	七	六	二	八	一	三	五	九
六	九	二	五	一	三	七	四	八
一	八	五	六	四	七	九	三	二
七	三	四	九	二	八	五	六	一
三	二	八	四	七	六	一	九	五
九	四	一	八	五	二	六	七	三
五	六	七	一	三	九	二	八	四

P. 51

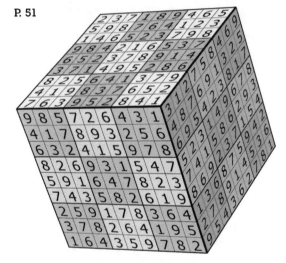

P. 52

P. 53

II	III	V	VIII	VI	I	VII	IX	IV
IV	VII	VI	II	III	IX	I	VIII	V
IX	VIII	I	V	VII	IV	VI	II	III
VIII	II	III	IX	IV	VII	V	I	VI
I	IV	IX	VI	V	VIII	II	III	VII
V	VI	VII	III	I	II	IX	IV	VIII
VII	IX	VIII	IV	II	VI	III	V	I
VI	V	II	I	VIII	III	IV	VII	IX
III	I	IV	VII	IX	V	VIII	VI	II

SOLUTIONS

P. 54

P. 55

P. 56

P. 57

8		2		3	1	6	4	5
7	5		4		6	9	3	
6	3	4		8		7		2
3	2		5	6	7		9	
1		5	8		4	2		3
	4		3	1	2		8	6
2		6		4		3	5	9
	1	3	6		9		2	7
5	8	9	2	7		4		1

P. 58

$	#	∧	⋆	(	@	!	&	%
!	⋆	@	$	&	%	#	∧	(
%	&	(	∧	!	#	$	⋆	@
⋆	!	$	(	∧	&	%	@	#
&	@	#	%	⋆	$	∧	(	!
∧	(	%	@	#	!	&	$	⋆
(	%	⋆	!	∧	\	@	#	&
#	$	!	&	@	(	⋆	%	∧
@	∧	&	#	%	⋆	(	!	$

P. 59

1.0079 H HYDROGEN	10.811 B BORON	4.0026 He HELIUM	12.011 C CARBON	9.0122 Be BERYLLIUM	6.941 Li LITHIUM	15.999 O OXYGEN	14.007 N NITROGEN	18.998 F FLUORINE
15.999 O OXYGEN	9.0122 Be BERYLLIUM	12.011 C CARBON	14.007 N NITROGEN	1.0079 H HYDROGEN	18.998 F FLUORINE	4.0026 He HELIUM	10.811 B BORON	6.941 Li LITHIUM
6.941 Li LITHIUM	18.998 F FLUORINE	14.007 N NITROGEN	4.0026 He HELIUM	10.811 B BORON	15.999 O OXYGEN	12.011 C CARBON	9.0122 Be BERYLLIUM	1.0079 H HYDROGEN
18.998 F FLUORINE	1.0079 H HYDROGEN	6.941 Li LITHIUM	15.999 O OXYGEN	14.007 N NITROGEN	10.811 B BORON	9.0122 Be BERYLLIUM	12.011 C CARBON	4.0026 He HELIUM
12.011 C CARBON	15.999 O OXYGEN	9.0122 Be BERYLLIUM	18.998 F FLUORINE	4.0026 He HELIUM	1.0079 H HYDROGEN	14.007 N NITROGEN	6.941 Li LITHIUM	10.811 B BORON
4.0026 He HELIUM	14.007 N NITROGEN	10.811 B BORON	9.0122 Be BERYLLIUM	6.941 Li LITHIUM	12.011 C CARBON	1.0079 H HYDROGEN	18.998 F FLUORINE	15.999 O OXYGEN
10.811 B BORON	4.0026 He HELIUM	1.0079 H HYDROGEN	6.941 Li LITHIUM	12.011 C CARBON	14.007 N NITROGEN	18.998 F FLUORINE	15.999 O OXYGEN	9.0122 Be BERYLLIUM
14.007 N NITROGEN	6.941 Li LITHIUM	18.998 F FLUORINE	1.0079 H HYDROGEN	15.999 O OXYGEN	9.0122 Be BERYLLIUM	10.811 B BORON	4.0026 He HELIUM	12.011 C CARBON
9.0122 Be BERYLLIUM	12.011 C CARBON	15.999 O OXYGEN	10.811 B BORON	18.998 F FLUORINE	4.0026 He HELIUM	6.941 Li LITHIUM	1.0079 H HYDROGEN	14.007 N NITROGEN

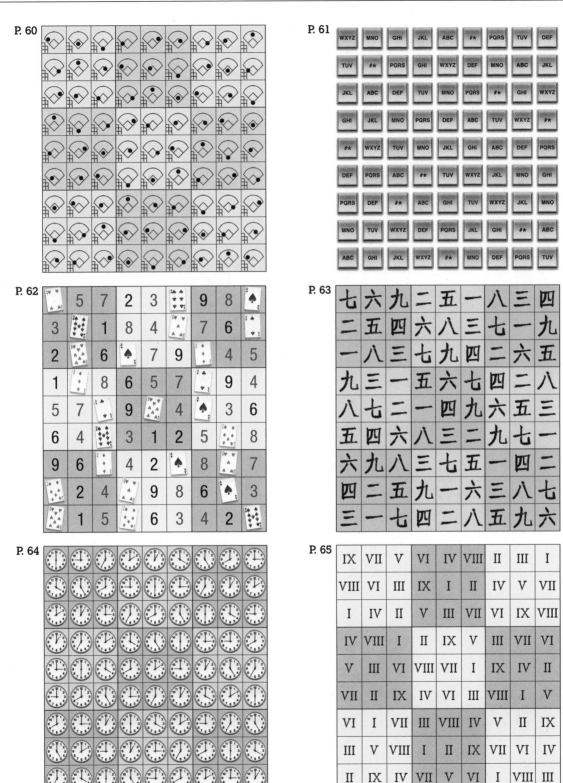

P. 60 P. 61 P. 62 P. 63 P. 64 P. 65

SOLUTIONS

P. 66

P. 67

P. 68

P. 69

1	3	4	2	8	🖐	🖐	6	7
7	9	✊	🖐	🖐	3	1	8	5
5	🖐	🖐	9	1	🖐	2	4	🖐
4	7	5	🖐	9	6	🖐	2	🖐
3	🖐	6	7	🖐	8	5	🖐	9
🖐	8	🖐	3	5	🖐	6	7	4
🖐	4	9	🖐	3	1	🖐	🖐	2
8	1	7	5	🖐	9	🖐	3	6
2	5	🖐	🖐	7	4	8	9	1

P. 70

P. 71

18.998 F FLUORINE	10.811 B BORON	12.011 C CARBON	4.0026 He HELIUM	14.007 N NITROGEN	1.0079 H HYDROGEN	9.0122 Be BERYLLIUM	15.999 O OXYGEN	6.941 Li LITHIUM
15.999 O OXYGEN	4.0026 He HELIUM	9.0122 Be BERYLLIUM	12.011 C CARBON	6.941 Li LITHIUM	10.811 B BORON	1.0079 H HYDROGEN	18.998 F FLUORINE	14.007 N NITROGEN
6.941 Li LITHIUM	1.0079 H HYDROGEN	14.007 N NITROGEN	9.0122 Be BERYLLIUM	15.999 O OXYGEN	18.998 F FLUORINE	12.011 C CARBON	10.811 B BORON	4.0026 He HELIUM
14.007 N NITROGEN	15.999 O OXYGEN	6.941 Li LITHIUM	1.0079 H HYDROGEN	10.811 B BORON	9.0122 Be BERYLLIUM	18.998 F FLUORINE	4.0026 He HELIUM	12.011 C CARBON
4.0026 He HELIUM	18.998 F FLUORINE	10.811 B BORON	15.999 O OXYGEN	12.011 C CARBON	6.941 Li LITHIUM	14.007 N NITROGEN	1.0079 H HYDROGEN	9.0122 Be BERYLLIUM
12.011 C CARBON	9.0122 Be BERYLLIUM	1.0079 H HYDROGEN	18.998 F FLUORINE	4.0026 He HELIUM	14.007 N NITROGEN	15.999 O OXYGEN	6.941 Li LITHIUM	10.811 B BORON
9.0122 Be BERYLLIUM	6.941 Li LITHIUM	18.998 F FLUORINE	14.007 N NITROGEN	1.0079 H HYDROGEN	4.0026 He HELIUM	10.811 B BORON	12.011 C CARBON	15.999 O OXYGEN
1.0079 H HYDROGEN	12.011 C CARBON	4.0026 He HELIUM	10.811 B BORON	9.0122 Be BERYLLIUM	15.999 O OXYGEN	6.941 Li LITHIUM	14.007 N NITROGEN	18.998 F FLUORINE
10.811 B BORON	14.007 N NITROGEN	15.999 O OXYGEN	6.941 Li LITHIUM	18.998 F FLUORINE	12.011 C CARBON	4.0026 He HELIUM	9.0122 Be BERYLLIUM	1.0079 H HYDROGEN

P. 72

P. 73

DEF	GHI	JKL	ABC	MNO	#★	TUV	PQRS	WXYZ
WXYZ	MNO	TUV	DEF	GHI	PQRS	#★	ABC	JKL
#★	PQRS	ABC	JKL	WXYZ	TUV	GHI	MNO	DEF
MNO	DEF	GHI	PQRS	TUV	WXYZ	JKL	#★	ABC
JKL	TUV	WXYZ	MNO	#★	ABC	DEF	GHI	PQRS
PQRS	ABC	#★	GHI	JKL	DEF	WXYZ	TUV	MNO
TUV	WXYZ	MNO	#★	ABC	JKL	PQRS	DEF	GHI
GHI	#★	PQRS	WXYZ	DEF	MNO	ABC	JKL	TUV
ABC	JKL	DEF	TUV	PQRS	GHI	MNO	WXYZ	#★

P. 74

7	8	2	9	♦	6	4	♠	5
3	4	6	1	5	♦	♣	9	8
1	♣	♣	8	4	2	6	3	7
♣	5	9	♣	1	3	♣	♣	4
♥	3	1	♦	8	♥	9	2	♥
2	♦	♥	6	9	♥	3	5	♠
8	6	7	3	2	1	♥	♦	9
9	2	♥	♦	7	8	1	6	3
5	♠	3	4	♣	9	8	7	2

P. 75

三	九	六	八	五	一	七	四	二
一	四	七	二	三	六	五	八	九
五	二	八	九	四	七	三	一	六
六	五	四	一	八	九	二	七	三
八	一	九	七	二	三	六	五	四
二	七	三	四	六	五	八	九	一
九	六	二	五	一	八	四	三	七
七	三	五	六	九	四	一	二	八
四	八	一	三	七	二	九	六	五

P. 76

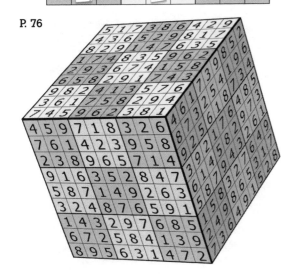

P. 77

SOLUTIONS

P. 78

VI	V	II	IV	IX	III	VIII	I	VII
IV	VIII	I	II	VI	VII	IX	V	III
IX	III	VII	VIII	I	V	IV	II	VI
II	IV	VI	IX	V	VIII	III	VII	I
III	I	V	VII	IV	II	VI	VIII	IX
VIII	VII	IX	VI	III	I	II	IV	V
V	IX	IV	I	VIII	VI	VII	III	II
VII	VI	III	V	II	IV	I	IX	VIII
I	II	VIII	III	VII	IX	V	VI	IV

P. 79

P. 80

P. 81

P. 82

5	7		9	8	1	2		6
4	9	2		3	7	5		
	8	6			5	3	7	9
3			1	7		8	6	4
8	1		3	5	6		9	2
9	6	7		4	2			5
6	3	9	5			4	2	
		8	7	6		9	5	1
7		1	2	9	4		8	3

P. 83

&	%	∧	⋆	#	$	(	@	!
!	$	⋆	@	(	%	#	∧	&
@	#	(	!	&	∧	%	⋆	$
%	@	&	#	∧	(	$	!	⋆
⋆	(	!	&	$	@	∧	%	#
#	∧	$	%	!	⋆	@	&	(
$	!	#	∧	@	&	⋆	(	%
(	⋆	@	$	%	!	&	#	∧
∧	&	%	(	⋆	#	!	$	@

P. 84

F	Li	B	H	Be	He	N	O	C
H	Be	C	B	N	O	F	Li	He
O	He	N	C	F	Li	Be	H	B
C	N	F	He	B	H	Li	Be	O
He	H	O	Be	Li	C	B	N	F
Be	B	Li	F	O	N	He	C	H
Li	O	H	N	He	B	C	F	Be
B	C	Be	Li	H	F	O	He	N
N	F	He	O	C	Be	H	B	Li

P. 85

P. 86

MNO	GHI	ABC	WXYZ	DEF	TUV	PQRS	#★	JKL
#★	PQRS	JKL	GHI	ABC	MNO	WXYZ	TUV	DEF
WXYZ	DEF	TUV	PQRS	JKL	#★	MNO	GHI	ABC
GHI	TUV	WXYZ	JKL	PQRS	DEF	#★	ABC	MNO
PQRS	ABC	#★	MNO	TUV	WXYZ	JKL	DEF	GHI
DEF	JKL	MNO	ABC	#★	GHI	TUV	WXYZ	PQRS
TUV	#★	PQRS	DEF	GHI	JKL	ABC	MNO	WXYZ
ABC	WXYZ	GHI	TUV	MNO	PQRS	DEF	JKL	#★
JKL	MNO	DEF	#★	WXYZ	ABC	GHI	PQRS	TUV

P. 87

P. 88

五	四	八	九	七	六	二	三	一
一	七	六	三	二	四	五	九	八
九	三	二	一	八	五	四	六	七
八	六	一	五	三	二	七	四	九
七	二	五	八	四	九	六	一	三
四	九	三	七	六	一	八	二	五
三	五	四	二	一	七	九	八	六
二	一	七	六	九	八	三	五	四
六	八	九	四	五	三	一	七	二

P. 89

SOLUTIONS

P. 90

III	VII	IX	I	II	V	VIII	IV	VI
V	IV	II	VII	VI	VIII	III	I	IX
I	VIII	VI	IV	IX	III	II	VII	V
VIII	II	V	III	VII	VI	IV	IX	I
VII	I	IV	IX	V	II	VI	VIII	III
VI	IX	III	VIII	I	IV	V	II	VII
II	III	I	VI	VIII	IX	VII	V	IV
IV	V	VII	II	III	I	IX	VI	VIII
IX	VI	VIII	V	IV	VII	I	III	II

P. 91

P. 92

P. 93

P. 94

2	6	3	1	7	4	9	3	5
8	7	5	3	4	6	2	4	1
1	4	9	5	2	7	1	3	8
5	8	1	3	7	9	4	2	3
4	3	7	6	4	1	5	8	3
3	3	1	8	3	4	4	9	6
3	4	3	4	6	2	1	5	4
7	5	2	9	4	8	3	4	4
6	1	4	7	5	5	8	2	9

P. 95

!	#	★	@	&	(	%	∧	$
&	$	∧	!	%	#	★	@	(
@	(	%	★	$	∧	&	#	!
%	★	$	#	∧	!	(	&	@
∧	&	@	$	(	★	!	%	#
(	!	#	&	@	%	∧	$	★
$	@	!	∧	★	&	#	(	%
#	%	&	(	!	@	$	★	∧
★	∧	(	%	#	$	@	!	&

P. 96

H	F	C	B	N	He	O	Be	Li
He	B	O	Li	Be	F	H	C	N
Li	Be	N	H	O	C	F	He	B
N	C	Be	F	He	Li	B	O	H
B	O	Li	C	H	Be	He	N	F
F	H	He	N	B	O	C	Li	Be
O	He	H	Be	Li	B	N	F	C
Be	N	F	O	C	H	Li	B	He
C	Li	B	He	F	N	Be	H	O

(Each cell also shows atomic weight and element name — e.g. 1.0079 H HYDROGEN, 18.998 F FLUORINE, 12.011 C CARBON, 10.811 B BORON, 14.007 N NITROGEN, 4.0026 He HELIUM, 15.999 O OXYGEN, 9.0122 Be BERYLLIUM, 6.941 Li LITHIUM.)

P. 97

(Baseball-diamond grid solution.)

P. 98

DEF	PQRS	WXYZ	GHI	JKL	MNO	#★	ABC	TUV
GHI	ABC	MNO	PQRS	#★	TUV	JKL	WXYZ	DEF
TUV	#★	JKL	DEF	ABC	WXYZ	PQRS	GHI	MNO
#★	MNO	ABC	TUV	WXYZ	GHI	DEF	PQRS	JKL
JKL	GHI	DEF	ABC	MNO	PQRS	WXYZ	TUV	#★
PQRS	WXYZ	TUV	#★	DEF	JKL	ABC	MNO	GHI
WXYZ	TUV	PQRS	JKL	GHI	#★	MNO	DEF	ABC
MNO	DEF	#★	WXYZ	TUV	ABC	GHI	JKL	PQRS
ABC	JKL	GHI	MNO	PQRS	DEF	TUV	#★	WXYZ

P. 99

8	9	5	7	1	3

(Playing-card sudoku solution, with number cells and card cells.)

P. 100

七	六	一	五	二	四	三	八	九
八	二	九	七	六	三	一	四	五
三	四	五	八	九	一	六	七	二
二	五	六	九	四	八	七	一	三
一	三	四	二	七	六	九	五	八
九	七	八	三	一	五	二	六	四
五	八	二	六	三	七	四	九	一
六	一	三	四	八	九	五	二	七
四	九	七	一	五	二	八	三	六

P. 101

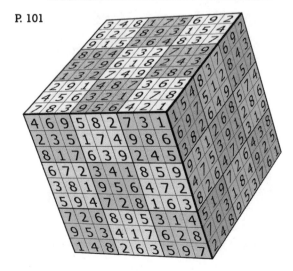

SOLUTIONS

P. 102

P. 103

V	VII	I	III	IX	II	VI	VIII	IV
IX	VI	III	IV	VIII	VII	I	II	V
II	IV	VIII	VI	V	I	IX	III	VII
I	V	IX	VIII	VII	III	II	IV	VI
VII	VIII	II	V	IV	VI	III	I	IX
IV	III	VI	I	II	IX	VII	V	VIII
III	II	IV	VII	VI	V	VIII	IX	I
VI	IX	V	II	I	VIII	IV	VII	III
VIII	I	VII	IX	III	IV	V	VI	II

P. 104

P. 105

P. 106

P. 107

		8	3	7		5	4	2
	2	5	6		9		3	1
7	1	3		2	4	8		9
8	3			1	5	4	9	
5		9	2		6	3		8
	4	6	8	9			7	5
3		1	4	6		9	8	7
2	9		1		8	6	5	
6	8	4		5	7	1		

272

P. 108

$	@	#	%	★	(	!	&	∧
!	∧	&	@	#	$	%	(	★
★	(	%	&	!	∧	@	#	$
(	#	★	!	$	&	∧	@	%
&	%	!	#	∧	@	★	$	(
∧	$	@	★	(	%	&	!	#
#	★	∧	(	&	!	$	%	@
@	!	$	∧	%	#	(	★	&
%	&	(	$	@	★	#	∧	!

P. 109

O	B	He	Be	F	H	N	Li	C
Be	Li	C	O	N	B	He	F	H
F	H	N	C	He	Li	O	B	Be
C	He	Be	H	Li	F	B	O	N
B	F	H	N	O	C	Be	He	Li
Li	N	O	B	Be	He	C	H	F
H	O	B	F	C	Be	Li	N	He
He	Be	F	Li	B	N	H	C	O
N	C	Li	He	H	O	F	Be	B

P. 110

P. 111

GHI	#★	JKL	ABC	TUV	MNO	PQRS	WXYZ	DEF
WXYZ	TUV	ABC	PQRS	JKL	DEF	#★	GHI	MNO
MNO	DEF	PQRS	GHI	#★	WXYZ	TUV	ABC	JKL
JKL	WXYZ	#★	MNO	DEF	PQRS	ABC	TUV	GHI
DEF	MNO	TUV	#★	ABC	GHI	JKL	PQRS	WXYZ
ABC	PQRS	GHI	JKL	WXYZ	TUV	DEF	MNO	#★
PQRS	JKL	WXYZ	TUV	GHI	#★	MNO	DEF	ABC
TUV	ABC	DEF	WXYZ	MNO	JKL	GHI	#★	PQRS
#★	GHI	MNO	DEF	PQRS	ABC	WXYZ	JKL	TUV

P. 112

P. 113

七	九	六	四	八	三	一	二	五
五	一	二	九	七	六	三	八	四
四	八	三	二	一	五	七	六	九
八	六	五	一	九	四	二	三	七
一	三	七	八	五	二	九	四	六
二	四	九	三	六	七	八	五	一
九	七	四	五	三	八	六	一	二
六	二	八	七	四	一	五	九	三
三	五	一	六	二	九	四	七	八

P. 114

P. 115

VI	VII	II	IV	III	IX	I	VIII	V
IX	VIII	I	VII	II	V	VI	III	IV
III	V	IV	I	VIII	VI	VII	II	IX
I	IX	III	VIII	VI	IV	V	VII	II
V	VI	VII	II	IX	III	IV	I	VIII
II	IV	VIII	V	I	VII	IX	VI	III
VIII	I	VI	IX	V	II	III	IV	VII
IV	II	IX	III	VII	I	VIII	V	VI
VII	III	V	VI	IV	VIII	II	IX	I

P. 116

P. 117

P. 118

P. 119

1			6	4	3	2	9	
4	3	2			9	7	6	8
		5	8	2			3	1
9	5			7	8	3		6
7	8	6	4		1	9	5	2
3		1	9	6			7	
8	6			1	2	5		
2	4	7	5			1	8	3
	1	3	7	8	4			9

P. 120

&	(	%	✶	∧	!	$	@	#
@	✶	#	$	%	(	&	!	∧
!	∧	$	&	#	@	(	%	✶
✶	&	@	(	$	%	#	∧	!
(	#	∧	!	@	&	✶	$	%
$	%	!	∧	✶	#	@	(	&
∧	!	(	@	&	✶	%	#	$
%	@	✶	#	!	$	∧	&	(
#	$	&	%	(	∧	!	✶	@

P. 121

F	N	H	Be	B	C	O	He	Li
O	Be	Li	H	F	He	B	N	C
B	He	C	O	Li	N	Be	H	F
Li	H	Be	F	N	O	He	C	B
N	F	He	C	H	B	Li	O	Be
C	O	B	He	Li	N	F	Be	H
Be	Li	O	N	C	H	F	B	He
H	C	N	B	He	Be	F	Li	O
He	B	F	Li	O	H	C	Be	N

P. 122

P. 123

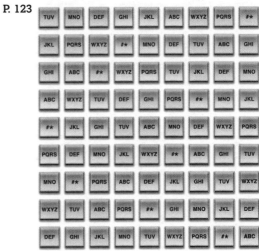

TUV	MNO	DEF	GHI	JKL	ABC	WXYZ	PQRS	#✶
JKL	PQRS	WXYZ	#✶	MNO	DEF	TUV	ABC	GHI
GHI	ABC	#✶	WXYZ	PQRS	TUV	JKL	DEF	MNO
ABC	WXYZ	TUV	DEF	GHI	PQRS	#✶	MNO	JKL
#✶	JKL	GHI	TUV	ABC	MNO	DEF	WXYZ	PQRS
PQRS	DEF	MNO	JKL	WXYZ	#✶	ABC	GHI	TUV
MNO	#✶	PQRS	ABC	DEF	JKL	GHI	TUV	WXYZ
WXYZ	TUV	ABC	PQRS	#✶	GHI	MNO	JKL	DEF
DEF	GHI	JKL	MNO	TUV	WXYZ	PQRS	#✶	ABC

P. 124

P. 125

四	七	九	三	六	八	二	五	一
二	五	八	四	七	一	三	六	九
一	三	六	九	二	五	八	七	四
七	一	五	六	四	二	九	三	八
六	八	四	一	九	三	七	二	五
九	二	三	八	五	七	四	一	六
八	九	一	七	三	六	五	四	二
三	四	二	五	一	九	六	八	七
五	六	七	二	八	四	一	九	三

SOLUTIONS

P. 126

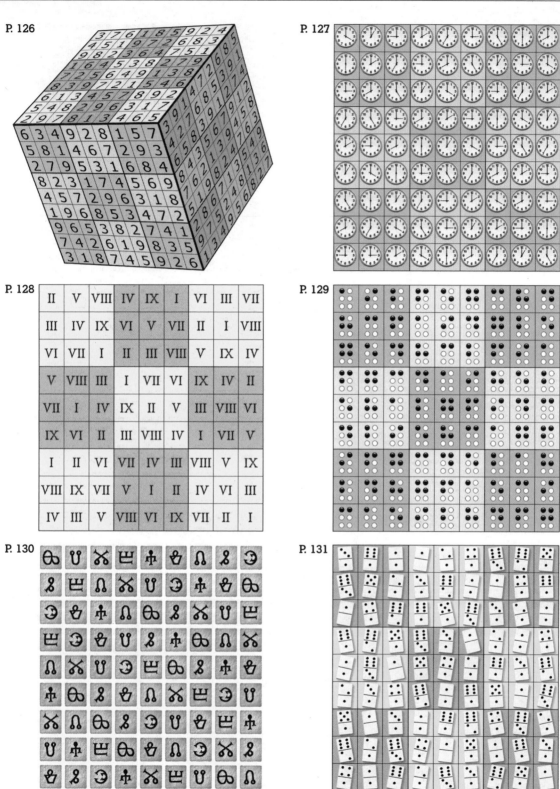

P. 127

P. 128

II	V	VIII	IV	IX	I	VI	III	VII
III	IV	IX	VI	V	VII	II	I	VIII
VI	VII	I	II	III	VIII	V	IX	IV
V	VIII	III	I	VII	VI	IX	IV	II
VII	I	IV	IX	II	V	III	VIII	VI
IX	VI	II	III	VIII	IV	I	VII	V
I	II	VI	VII	IV	III	VIII	V	IX
VIII	IX	VII	V	I	II	IV	VI	III
IV	III	V	VIII	VI	IX	VII	II	I

P. 129

P. 130

P. 131

P. 132

6	7	[hand]	2	3	4	8	[hand]	[hand]
8	[hand]	2	[hand]	9	5	7	4	[hand]
[hand]	1	[hand]	7	[hand]	6	9	3	2
9	[hand]	6	[hand]	5	1	2	7	4
5	4	[hand]	6	[hand]	8	[hand]	1	9
1	2	3	4	7	[hand]	5	[hand]	8
7	9	1	8	[hand]	3	[hand]	2	[hand]
[hand]	5	4	9	6	[hand]	[hand]	1	3
[hand]	[hand]	8	5	1	2	[hand]	9	7

P. 133

#	&	(	*	!	%	∧	$	@
*	$	%	∧	#	@	&	!	(
@	∧	!	&	$	(	*	#	%
(	!	∧	%	*	&	#	@	$
&	%	@	#	∧	$	!	(	*
$	*	#	(	@	!	%	&	∧
!	(	&	@	%	∧	$	*	#
∧	#	$	!	(	*	@	%	&
%	@	*	$	&	#	(	∧	!

P. 134

C CARBON	F FLUORINE	O OXYGEN	H HYDROGEN	Li LITHIUM	He HELIUM	Be BERYLLIUM	B BORON	N NITROGEN
Li LITHIUM	B BORON	H HYDROGEN	O OXYGEN	N NITROGEN	Be BERYLLIUM	F FLUORINE	He HELIUM	C CARBON
Be BERYLLIUM	He HELIUM	N NITROGEN	C CARBON	B BORON	F FLUORINE	O OXYGEN	Li LITHIUM	H HYDROGEN
B BORON	N NITROGEN	F FLUORINE	Be BERYLLIUM	O OXYGEN	Li LITHIUM	C CARBON	H HYDROGEN	He HELIUM
He HELIUM	H HYDROGEN	C CARBON	B BORON	F FLUORINE	N NITROGEN	Li LITHIUM	O OXYGEN	Be BERYLLIUM
O OXYGEN	Li LITHIUM	Be BERYLLIUM	He HELIUM	H HYDROGEN	C CARBON	N NITROGEN	F FLUORINE	B BORON
F FLUORINE	O OXYGEN	He HELIUM	N NITROGEN	C CARBON	H HYDROGEN	B BORON	Be BERYLLIUM	Li LITHIUM
H HYDROGEN	C CARBON	B BORON	Li LITHIUM	Be BERYLLIUM	O OXYGEN	He HELIUM	N NITROGEN	F FLUORINE
N NITROGEN	Be BERYLLIUM	Li LITHIUM	F FLUORINE	He HELIUM	B BORON	H HYDROGEN	C CARBON	O OXYGEN

P. 135

(grid of baseball diamond symbols)

P. 136

#*	ABC	PQRS	MNO	JKL	DEF	TUV	GHI	WXYZ
MNO	WXYZ	JKL	#*	GHI	TUV	ABC	DEF	PQRS
DEF	TUV	GHI	ABC	PQRS	WXYZ	MNO	JKL	#*
ABC	JKL	MNO	TUV	WXYZ	PQRS	DEF	#*	GHI
WXYZ	PQRS	DEF	GHI	MNO	#*	JKL	TUV	ABC
TUV	GHI	#*	DEF	ABC	JKL	PQRS	WXYZ	MNO
PQRS	MNO	WXYZ	JKL	TUV	GHI	#*	ABC	DEF
GHI	#*	TUV	PQRS	DEF	ABC	WXYZ	MNO	JKL
JKL	DEF	ABC	WXYZ	#*	MNO	GHI	PQRS	TUV

P. 137

8	[card]	7	[card]	1	9	2	5	4
5	4	[card]	8	[card]	2	[card]	6	[card]
2	[card]	1	[card]	5	6	9	[card]	7
3	2	8	5	4	1	[card]	7	[card]
6	[card]	4	9	[card]	8	5	[card]	1
[card]	9	[card]	6	3	7	8	4	2
7	[card]	2	1	6	[card]	3	[card]	5
[card]	5	[card]	2	[card]	3	[card]	1	8
9	1	3	7	8	[card]	4	[card]	6

SOLUTIONS

P. 138

八	二	五	四	七	六	九	三	一
九	四	六	一	三	二	八	五	七
三	七	一	五	八	九	六	二	四
一	六	二	七	九	三	五	四	八
七	五	三	八	四	一	二	六	九
四	九	八	六	二	五	七	一	三
六	一	四	九	五	八	三	七	二
二	八	七	三	六	四	一	九	五
五	三	九	二	一	七	四	八	六

P. 139

P. 140

V	I	III	II	VII	VIII	VI	IX	IV
IV	IX	VIII	III	VI	I	V	II	VII
VI	VII	II	IV	IX	V	III	VIII	I
III	II	I	VI	IV	IX	VII	V	VIII
VIII	VI	IX	VII	V	III	I	IV	II
VII	IV	V	I	VIII	II	IX	VI	III
II	VIII	VI	IX	III	VII	IV	I	V
I	III	IV	V	II	VI	VIII	VII	IX
IX	V	VII	VIII	I	IV	II	III	VI

P. 141

P. 142

P. 143

P. 144

6	[hand]	3	[hand]	4	9	[hand]	8	5
2	[hand]	4	1	[hand]	[hand]	3	9	7
[hand]	7	8	3	2	5	6	1	[hand]
7	9	[hand]	[hand]	1	3	8	4	[hand]
4	[hand]	5	6	[hand]	7	9	[hand]	1
[hand]	3	1	2	9	[hand]	[hand]	5	6
[hand]	4	7	9	5	6	1	2	[hand]
1	8	9	[hand]	[hand]	2	5	[hand]	3
5	6	[hand]	8	3	[hand]	[hand]	4	9

P. 145

✱	$	&	!	@	%	∧	(	#
!	@	∧	&	(	#	✱	%	$
(	%	#	$	✱	∧	&	!	@
@	!	(	∧	$	✱	#	&	%
#	∧	%	(	!	&	@	$	✱
$	&	✱	%	#	@	!	∧	(
&	✱	$	#	∧	(	%	@	!
%	#	!	@	&	$	(	✱	∧
∧	(	@	✱	%	!	$	#	&

P. 146

F	N	O	B	Li	Be	H	C	He
B	H	He	N	F	C	Li	O	Be
Be	Li	C	He	O	H	N	F	B
C	B	Li	H	N	He	O	Be	F
O	F	H	Li	Be	B	He	N	C
He	Be	N	O	C	F	B	Li	H
Li	He	Be	C	B	O	F	H	N
H	O	F	Be	He	N	C	B	Li
N	C	B	F	H	Li	Be	He	O

P. 147

P. 148

ABC	DEF	MNO	#✱	PQRS	TUV	JKL	GHI	WXYZ
JKL	PQRS	#✱	DEF	GHI	WXYZ	ABC	TUV	MNO
GHI	WXYZ	TUV	JKL	MNO	ABC	#✱	PQRS	DEF
PQRS	MNO	JKL	WXYZ	DEF	GHI	TUV	ABC	#✱
WXYZ	ABC	GHI	TUV	#✱	JKL	DEF	MNO	PQRS
#✱	TUV	DEF	PQRS	ABC	MNO	WXYZ	JKL	GHI
MNO	JKL	ABC	GHI	WXYZ	DEF	PQRS	#✱	TUV
DEF	GHI	PQRS	ABC	TUV	#✱	MNO	WXYZ	JKL
TUV	#✱	WXYZ	MNO	JKL	PQRS	GHI	DEF	ABC

P. 149

7	[card]	9	4	5	[card]	6	[card]	8
[card]	5	4	3	[card]	9	2	1	[card]
3	8	2	7	1	[card]	5	9	4
1	3	[card]	[card]	4	8	9	2	[card]
4	9	[card]	[card]	2	[card]	[card]	7	5
[card]	6	5	9	3	[card]	[card]	8	1
5	7	3	[card]	9	4	8	6	2
[card]	4	1	2	[card]	3	7	5	[card]
9	[card]	6	[card]	7	5	1	[card]	3

P. 150

九	七	二	六	三	八	五	一	四
四	八	六	七	五	一	九	三	二
五	一	三	九	二	四	六	七	八
二	五	七	三	八	六	一	四	九
三	四	八	五	一	九	二	六	七
六	九	一	二	四	七	八	五	三
七	六	五	四	九	二	三	八	一
八	二	四	一	六	三	七	九	五
一	三	九	八	七	五	四	二	六

P. 151

P. 152

P. 153

IV	VII	IX	II	III	I	V	VI	VIII
I	VIII	II	VI	V	IX	IV	III	VII
VI	V	III	VIII	IV	VII	II	IX	I
IX	I	V	III	VII	IV	VIII	II	VI
III	VI	VII	IX	VIII	II	I	V	IV
II	IV	VIII	V	I	VI	III	VII	IX
VII	II	IV	I	VI	III	IX	VIII	V
V	III	VI	IV	IX	VIII	VII	I	II
VIII	IX	I	VII	II	V	VI	IV	III

P. 154

P. 155

P. 156

P. 157

		5	9	8		2	6	
	7	3	2		6	1		4
9	6		4	1	3		7	8
6	3	1	7	9		4	8	
5		9	6		1	7		2
	2	4		3	5	9	1	6
1	4		3	2	9		5	7
3		7	5		4	8	2	
	5	6		7	8	3		

P. 158

&	✶	(	∧	#	$	%	@	!
!	∧	%	@	✶	&	#	$	(
#	$	@	(	!	%	&	∧	✶
∧	@	!	#	&	✶	$	(	%
$	(	#	!	%	@	✶	&	∧
%	&	✶	$	(	∧	@	!	#
@	!	&	%	∧	#	(	✶	$
(	%	$	✶	@	!	∧	#	&
✶	#	∧	&	$	(	!	%	@

P. 159

Li	C	B	He	O	Be	F	N	H
O	H	F	N	Li	B	He	C	Be
Be	N	He	C	F	H	O	B	Li
B	F	C	Li	He	O	H	Be	N
He	O	H	B	Be	N	C	Li	F
N	Li	Be	H	C	F	B	He	O
F	B	Li	O	N	He	Be	H	C
C	He	O	Be	H	Li	N	F	B
H	Be	N	F	B	C	Li	O	He

P. 160

P. 161

GHI	MNO	TUV	#★	PQRS	JKL	DEF	WXYZ	ABC
ABC	JKL	DEF	MNO	WXYZ	GHI	PQRS	#★	TUV
#★	WXYZ	PQRS	DEF	TUV	ABC	JKL	GHI	MNO
TUV	PQRS	#★	JKL	DEF	MNO	WXYZ	ABC	GHI
DEF	ABC	JKL	WXYZ	GHI	#★	MNO	TUV	PQRS
WXYZ	GHI	MNO	TUV	ABC	PQRS	#★	DEF	JKL
JKL	DEF	WXYZ	GHI	MNO	TUV	ABC	PQRS	#★
MNO	TUV	ABC	PQRS	#★	WXYZ	GHI	JKL	DEF
PQRS	#★	GHI	ABC	JKL	DEF	TUV	MNO	WXYZ

P. 162

P. 163

二	七	三	五	一	四	六	九	八
六	八	五	三	九	七	四	二	一
一	九	四	二	六	八	五	三	七
七	三	六	九	八	五	二	一	四
五	四	一	七	二	三	八	六	九
八	二	九	六	四	一	七	五	三
四	六	二	一	七	九	三	八	五
九	五	七	八	三	六	一	四	二
三	一	八	四	五	二	九	七	六

P. 164

P. 165

III	VIII	VI	II	IV	I	V	VII	IX
V	I	IX	VI	VIII	VII	III	IV	II
II	IV	VII	IX	III	V	I	VIII	VI
IX	II	IV	I	VII	VI	VIII	V	III
VI	III	VIII	IV	V	II	IX	I	VII
I	VII	V	III	IX	VIII	II	VI	IV
VIII	IX	III	V	VI	IV	VII	II	I
VII	VI	I	VIII	II	IX	IV	III	V
IV	V	II	VII	I	III	VI	IX	VIII

P. 166

P. 167

P. 168

P. 169

3	4	✌	2	5	✌	6	8	✌
1	✋	6	4	✌	7	2	✌	5
✌	5	9	✋	1	8	✌	4	3
8	2	✋	1	4	6	9	3	7
9	6	✋	7	✌	3	✋	1	8
4	✌	1	8	9	5	✋	6	2
7	1	✋	5	6	✌	8	3	✌
5	✋	2	9	✋	4	1	✋	6
✋	9	8	✌	7	1	✋	2	4

P. 170

&	%	#	(	★	!	$	@	∧
★	$	(	∧	@	&	%	#	!
∧	!	@	$	#	%	(	★	&
$	(	∧	#	&	@	!	%	★
%	@	!	★	(	$	&	∧	#
#	&	★	%	!	∧	@	(	$
@	∧	$	!	%	#	★	&	(
!	★	%	&	∧	(	#	$	@
(	#	&	@	$	★	∧	!	%

P. 171

He	H	F	O	Li	N	Be	C	B
N	C	Li	H	B	Be	O	He	F
Be	O	B	He	F	C	Li	H	N
Li	N	O	F	Be	H	C	B	He
C	F	He	B	N	Li	H	O	Be
B	Be	H	C	O	He	N	F	Li
O	He	N	Li	C	B	F	Be	H
F	B	Be	N	H	O	He	Li	C
H	Li	C	Be	He	F	B	N	O

P. 172

P. 173

ABC	TUV	MNO	DEF	JKL	GHI	#★	WXYZ	PQRS
JKL	DEF	WXYZ	PQRS	#★	TUV	ABC	GHI	MNO
GHI	#★	PQRS	WXYZ	ABC	MNO	TUV	JKL	DEF
TUV	GHI	#★	MNO	PQRS	DEF	JKL	ABC	WXYZ
PQRS	WXYZ	JKL	TUV	GHI	ABC	DEF	MNO	#★
DEF	MNO	ABC	JKL	WXYZ	#★	PQRS	TUV	GHI
WXYZ	JKL	GHI	#★	TUV	PQRS	MNO	DEF	ABC
MNO	PQRS	TUV	ABC	DEF	WXYZ	GHI	#★	JKL
#★	ABC	DEF	GHI	MNO	JKL	WXYZ	PQRS	TUV

P. 174

P. 175

三	四	五	二	一	九	七	六	八
二	七	六	八	五	三	一	四	九
八	一	九	四	七	六	三	二	五
四	五	二	一	三	八	九	七	六
一	六	七	九	二	四	八	五	三
九	八	三	五	六	七	二	一	四
五	二	四	三	八	一	六	九	七
六	九	八	七	四	二	五	三	一
七	三	一	六	九	五	四	八	二

P. 176

P. 177

P. 178

VII	VI	VIII	V	I	II	IX	IV	III
II	V	III	IX	VI	IV	VII	VIII	I
IX	IV	I	VIII	VII	III	II	VI	V
III	VIII	IV	II	IX	VII	I	V	VI
V	IX	VII	VI	IV	I	III	II	VIII
VI	I	II	III	V	VIII	IV	IX	VII
I	VII	VI	IV	II	V	VIII	III	IX
VIII	II	IX	VII	III	VI	V	I	IV
IV	III	V	I	VIII	IX	VI	VII	II

P. 179

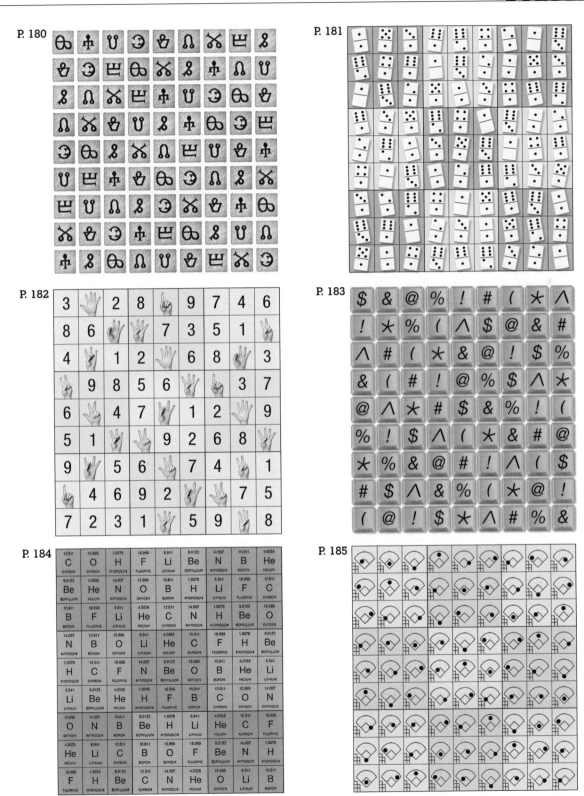

P. 180

P. 181

P. 182

P. 183

P. 184

P. 185

SOLUTIONS

P. 186

ABC	#★	JKL	TUV	WXYZ	PQRS	DEF	MNO	GHI
GHI	TUV	DEF	ABC	JKL	MNO	PQRS	WXYZ	#★
MNO	WXYZ	PQRS	GHI	#★	DEF	ABC	TUV	JKL
WXYZ	MNO	ABC	JKL	PQRS	GHI	#★	DEF	TUV
DEF	JKL	GHI	#★	TUV	ABC	MNO	PQRS	WXYZ
#★	PQRS	TUV	DEF	MNO	WXYZ	GHI	JKL	ABC
TUV	ABC	WXYZ	MNO	DEF	#★	JKL	GHI	PQRS
PQRS	GHI	MNO	WXYZ	ABC	JKL	TUV	#★	DEF
JKL	DEF	#★	PQRS	GHI	TUV	WXYZ	ABC	MNO

P. 187

P. 188

一	四	五	二	七	三	九	六	八
三	六	八	四	九	五	一	七	二
七	九	二	六	八	一	四	五	三
六	二	九	七	四	八	三	一	五
四	一	七	五	三	六	二	八	九
五	八	三	一	二	九	六	四	七
二	五	六	三	一	七	八	九	四
八	三	一	九	五	四	七	二	六
九	七	四	八	六	二	五	三	一

P. 189

P. 190

VI	III	VIII	IX	IV	VII	V	I	II
I	IV	IX	II	VI	V	VII	VIII	III
VII	V	II	III	VIII	I	VI	IV	IX
IV	VI	III	I	IX	VIII	II	V	VII
IX	II	VII	IV	V	VI	I	III	VIII
V	VIII	I	VII	II	III	IV	IX	VI
III	IX	VI	V	VII	IV	VIII	II	I
II	VII	IV	VIII	I	IX	III	VI	V
VIII	I	V	VI	III	II	IX	VII	IV

P. 191

P. 192

P. 193

P. 194

8		9	4	7	1	6		5
7	3	6	8		2	1	9	4
1	4			3			2	8
	6	7	2		4	5	1	
2		4		9		3		7
	5	8	3		7	2	4	
5	8			4			6	1
4	9	3	1		5	8	7	2
6		1	9	2	8	4		3

P. 195

★	&	@	!	%	#	(	$	∧
!	(	∧	&	$	@	#	★	%
$	%	#	★	∧	(	!	@	&
%	!	$	∧	@	&	★	#	(
(	#	&	%	★	!	$	∧	@
∧	@	★	(	#	$	%	&	!
&	$	%	#	!	∧	@	(	★
@	★	(	$	&	%	∧	!	#
#	∧	!	@	(	★	&	%	$

P. 196

15.999 O OXYGEN	18.998 F FLUORINE	6.941 Li LITHIUM	1.0079 H HYDROGEN	9.0122 Be BERYLLIUM	14.007 N NITROGEN	4.0026 He HELIUM	12.011 C CARBON	10.811 B BORON
10.811 B BORON	14.007 N NITROGEN	4.0026 He HELIUM	12.011 C CARBON	6.941 Li LITHIUM	15.999 O OXYGEN	1.0079 H HYDROGEN	18.998 F FLUORINE	9.0122 Be BERYLLIUM
9.0122 Be BERYLLIUM	1.0079 H HYDROGEN	12.011 C CARBON	18.998 F FLUORINE	10.811 B BORON	4.0026 He HELIUM	14.007 N NITROGEN	6.941 Li LITHIUM	15.999 O OXYGEN
18.998 F FLUORINE	6.941 Li LITHIUM	14.007 N NITROGEN	15.999 O OXYGEN	12.011 C CARBON	9.0122 Be BERYLLIUM	10.811 B BORON	4.0026 He HELIUM	1.0079 H HYDROGEN
4.0026 He HELIUM	15.999 O OXYGEN	9.0122 Be BERYLLIUM	10.811 B BORON	1.0079 H HYDROGEN	18.998 F FLUORINE	6.941 Li LITHIUM	14.007 N NITROGEN	12.011 C CARBON
1.0079 H HYDROGEN	12.011 C CARBON	10.811 B BORON	4.0026 He HELIUM	14.007 N NITROGEN	6.941 Li LITHIUM	15.999 O OXYGEN	9.0122 Be BERYLLIUM	18.998 F FLUORINE
12.011 C CARBON	4.0026 He HELIUM	1.0079 H HYDROGEN	14.007 N NITROGEN	18.998 F FLUORINE	10.811 B BORON	9.0122 Be BERYLLIUM	15.999 O OXYGEN	6.941 Li LITHIUM
6.941 Li LITHIUM	10.811 B BORON	15.999 O OXYGEN	9.0122 Be BERYLLIUM	4.0026 He HELIUM	12.011 C CARBON	18.998 F FLUORINE	1.0079 H HYDROGEN	14.007 N NITROGEN
14.007 N NITROGEN	9.0122 Be BERYLLIUM	18.998 F FLUORINE	6.941 Li LITHIUM	15.999 O OXYGEN	1.0079 H HYDROGEN	12.011 C CARBON	10.811 B BORON	4.0026 He HELIUM

P. 197

SOLUTIONS

P. 198

#★	GHI	PQRS	DEF	MNO	TUV	ABC	WXYZ	JKL
WXYZ	MNO	DEF	ABC	JKL	GHI	TUV	PQRS	#★
JKL	TUV	ABC	WXYZ	PQRS	#★	MNO	DEF	GHI
PQRS	JKL	#★	MNO	TUV	WXYZ	GHI	ABC	DEF
GHI	ABC	WXYZ	#★	DEF	PQRS	JKL	TUV	MNO
TUV	DEF	MNO	JKL	GHI	ABC	PQRS	#★	WXYZ
MNO	PQRS	JKL	TUV	WXYZ	DEF	#★	GHI	ABC
ABC	WXYZ	TUV	GHI	#★	JKL	DEF	MNO	PQRS
DEF	#★	GHI	PQRS	ABC	MNO	WXYZ	JKL	TUV

P. 199

2	7	5	8	3	6	9	4	1
8	1	9	7	4	5	2	3	6
4	6	3	9	1	2	5	8	7
9	5	8	2	6	3	7	1	4
1	3	6	5	7	4	8	2	9
7	2	4	1	9	8	3	6	5
3	9	1	6	8	7	4	5	2
5	4	7	3	2	1	6	9	8
6	8	2	4	5	9	1	7	3

P. 200

四	二	一	七	三	八	六	五	九
六	八	三	五	一	九	二	四	七
七	九	五	四	二	六	三	一	八
八	五	七	三	六	一	九	二	四
九	三	六	二	七	四	一	八	五
二	一	四	八	九	五	七	六	三
三	四	二	六	八	七	五	九	一
五	六	九	一	四	三	八	七	二
一	七	八	九	五	二	四	三	六

P. 201

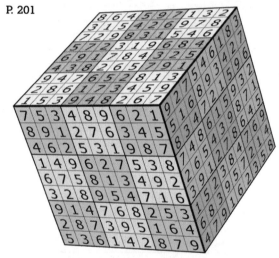

P. 202

P. 203

IX	II	IV	V	VI	I	VIII	III	VII
VI	VIII	I	IV	III	VII	IX	V	II
V	VII	III	II	VIII	IX	IV	VI	I
III	V	VII	I	IV	VI	II	IX	VIII
II	IX	VI	VIII	VII	V	I	IV	III
IV	I	VIII	III	IX	II	VI	VII	V
VIII	IV	V	IX	I	III	VII	II	VI
I	VI	II	VII	V	IV	III	VIII	IX
VII	III	IX	VI	II	VIII	V	I	IV

P. 204

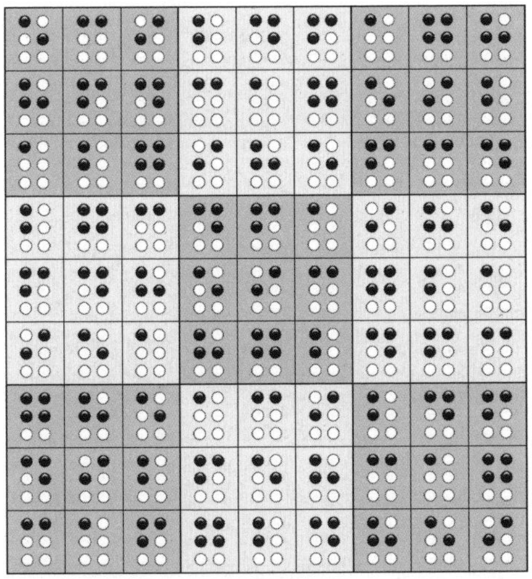

P. 205

P. 206

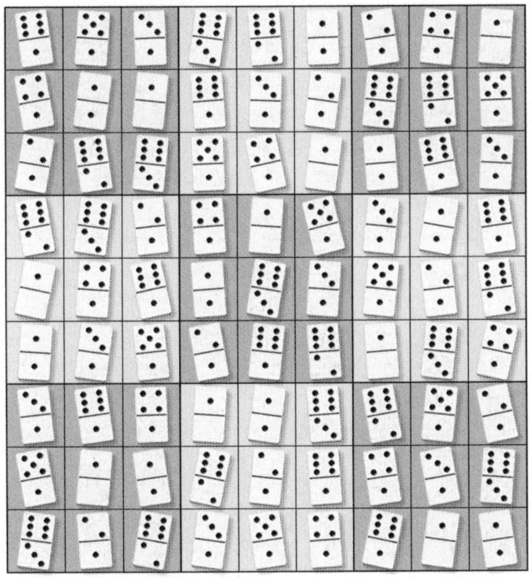

P. 207

P. 208

!	%	#	&	@	*	(	^	$
$	^	&	%	#	(	@	!	*
@	(	*	$	!	^	&	%	#
^	#	(	@	*	%	$	&	!
&	!	@	#	^	$	*	(	%
%	*	$	!	(	&	#	@	^
(	&	!	*	%	#	^	$	@
*	@	^	(	$	!	%	#	&
#	$	%	^	&	@	!	*	(

P. 209

14.007 N NITROGEN	1.0079 H HYDROGEN	18.998 F FLUORINE	4.0026 He HELIUM	10.811 B BORON	9.0122 Be BERYLLIUM	12.011 C CARBON	15.999 O OXYGEN	6.941 Li LITHIUM
9.0122 Be BERYLLIUM	10.811 B BORON	4.0026 He HELIUM	15.999 O OXYGEN	6.941 Li LITHIUM	12.011 C CARBON	14.007 N NITROGEN	1.0079 H HYDROGEN	18.998 F FLUORINE
15.999 O OXYGEN	6.941 Li LITHIUM	12.011 C CARBON	18.998 F FLUORINE	14.007 N NITROGEN	1.0079 H HYDROGEN	10.811 B BORON	4.0026 He HELIUM	9.0122 Be BERYLLIUM
12.011 C CARBON	18.998 F FLUORINE	6.941 Li LITHIUM	14.007 N NITROGEN	1.0079 H HYDROGEN	15.999 O OXYGEN	4.0026 He HELIUM	9.0122 Be BERYLLIUM	10.811 B BORON
10.811 B BORON	14.007 N NITROGEN	1.0079 H HYDROGEN	6.941 Li LITHIUM	9.0122 Be BERYLLIUM	4.0026 He HELIUM	18.998 F FLUORINE	12.011 C CARBON	15.999 O OXYGEN
4.0026 He HELIUM	15.999 O OXYGEN	9.0122 Be BERYLLIUM	12.011 C CARBON	18.998 F FLUORINE	10.811 B BORON	1.0079 H HYDROGEN	6.941 Li LITHIUM	14.007 N NITROGEN
1.0079 H HYDROGEN	12.011 C CARBON	14.007 N NITROGEN	9.0122 Be BERYLLIUM	15.999 O OXYGEN	18.998 F FLUORINE	6.941 Li LITHIUM	10.811 B BORON	4.0026 He HELIUM
6.941 Li LITHIUM	9.0122 Be BERYLLIUM	10.811 B BORON	1.0079 H HYDROGEN	4.0026 He HELIUM	14.007 N NITROGEN	15.999 O OXYGEN	18.998 F FLUORINE	12.011 C CARBON
18.998 F FLUORINE	4.0026 He HELIUM	15.999 O OXYGEN	10.811 B BORON	12.011 C CARBON	6.941 Li LITHIUM	9.0122 Be BERYLLIUM	14.007 N NITROGEN	1.0079 H HYDROGEN

SOLUTIONS

P. 210

P. 211

TUV	#★	GHI	ABC	DEF	MNO	WXYZ	JKL	PQRS
ABC	MNO	JKL	WXYZ	PQRS	TUV	#★	DEF	GHI
DEF	WXYZ	PQRS	JKL	GHI	#★	ABC	TUV	MNO
MNO	DEF	#★	GHI	ABC	WXYZ	JKL	PQRS	TUV
JKL	GHI	TUV	MNO	#★	PQRS	DEF	ABC	WXYZ
PQRS	ABC	WXYZ	TUV	JKL	DEF	MNO	GHI	#★
GHI	JKL	MNO	#★	TUV	ABC	PQRS	WXYZ	DEF
#★	PQRS	ABC	DEF	WXYZ	GHI	TUV	MNO	JKL
WXYZ	TUV	DEF	PQRS	MNO	JKL	GHI	#★	ABC

P. 212

P. 213

三	六	九	八	五	七	一	四	二
二	五	八	一	三	四	九	七	六
四	一	七	二	六	九	三	八	五
一	二	四	三	九	八	六	五	七
八	三	六	四	七	五	二	一	九
七	九	五	六	二	一	四	三	八
五	八	三	九	四	六	七	二	一
六	七	二	五	一	三	八	九	四
九	四	一	七	八	二	五	六	三

P. 214

P. 215

IV	IX	II	I	VIII	VI	V	III	VII
VI	V	VIII	VII	IX	III	IV	II	I
I	VII	III	II	IV	V	VIII	VI	IX
III	VIII	VII	IX	V	IV	VI	I	II
II	I	IX	VIII	VI	VII	III	V	IV
V	VI	IV	III	II	I	VII	IX	VIII
IX	III	V	IV	VII	II	I	VIII	VI
VII	II	VI	V	I	VIII	IX	IV	III
VIII	IV	I	VI	III	IX	II	VII	V

P. 216

P. 217

P. 218

P. 219

P. 220

P. 221

P. 222

P. 223

ABC	PQRS	MNO	DEF	TUV	WXYZ	GHI	JKL	#★
DEF	JKL	#★	GHI	MNO	ABC	TUV	PQRS	WXYZ
WXYZ	GHI	TUV	#★	JKL	PQRS	DEF	MNO	ABC
TUV	ABC	WXYZ	PQRS	#★	JKL	MNO	GHI	DEF
JKL	MNO	GHI	TUV	WXYZ	DEF	#★	ABC	PQRS
PQRS	#★	DEF	MNO	ABC	GHI	WXYZ	TUV	JKL
GHI	WXYZ	PQRS	ABC	DEF	TUV	JKL	#★	MNO
MNO	DEF	ABC	JKL	GHI	#★	PQRS	WXYZ	TUV
#★	TUV	JKL	WXYZ	PQRS	MNO	ABC	DEF	GHI

P. 224

9	♥	5	♥	6	7	3	1	2
♦	3	♠	2	♦	5	6	8	4
♣	6	8	4	♦	1	5	9	7
8	♥	7	♥	2	9	4	3	1
4	2	♣	1	8	3	♦	5	6
3	1	6	7	5	♥	9	♥	8
5	8	4	3	♠	6	2	7	♥
6	9	2	5	♦	8	♠	4	♦
1	7	3	9	4	♣	8	♣	5

P. 225

五	四	六	九	三	八	二	一	七
七	九	三	二	四	一	六	五	八
一	八	二	七	六	五	四	九	三
九	七	五	八	二	四	一	三	六
二	三	四	六	一	九	七	八	五
六	一	八	三	五	七	九	二	四
三	二	七	一	八	六	五	四	九
四	六	一	五	九	三	八	七	二
八	五	九	四	七	二	三	六	一

P. 226

P. 227

P. 228

I	VIII	III	IV	VI	V	IX	II	VII
V	IV	II	VII	I	IX	III	VIII	VI
IX	VI	VII	II	III	VIII	V	IV	I
IV	IX	V	VI	II	I	VIII	VII	III
VI	VII	VIII	III	V	IV	II	I	IX
III	II	I	IX	VIII	VII	IV	VI	V
VIII	III	IX	I	IV	VI	VII	V	II
II	I	IV	V	VII	III	VI	IX	VIII
VII	V	VI	VIII	IX	II	I	III	IV

P. 229

P. 230

P. 231

P. 232

7	5	1	8	3	6	2	9	4
3	6	2	4	9	1	7	3	5
4	9	8	7	5	2	1	3	6
6	3	7	5	1	2	9	4	8
9	1	4	6	8	3	5	7	2
8	2	5	9	7	4	3	6	1
1	4	6	3	2	5	8	2	9
5	8	3	2	6	9	4	1	7
2	7	9	1	4	8	6	5	3

P. 233

✶	&	∧	#	$	%	@	(	!
%	(	$	✶	@	!	&	∧	#
@	!	#	(	∧	&	$	✶	%
#	∧	&	@	(	✶	%	!	$
(	✶	%	!	&	$	#	@	∧
$	@	!	∧	%	#	(	&	✶
&	#	@	%	!	∧	✶	$	(
!	%	(	$	✶	@	∧	#	&
∧	$	✶	&	#	(	!	%	@

SOLUTIONS

P. 234

C 12.011	H 1.0079	Be 9.0122	O 15.999	F 18.998	N 14.007	He 4.0026	B 10.811	Li 6.941
B 10.811	O 15.999	F 18.998	Be 9.0122	Li 6.941	He 4.0026	N 14.007	H 1.0079	C 12.011
Li 6.941	N 14.007	He 4.0026	C 12.011	B 10.811	H 1.0079	O 15.999	Be 9.0122	F 18.998
H 1.0079	Li 6.941	B 10.811	He 4.0026	O 15.999	Be 9.0122	F 18.998	C 12.011	N 14.007
O 15.999	Be 9.0122	C 12.011	B 10.811	N 14.007	F 18.998	H 1.0079	Li 6.941	He 4.0026
He 4.0026	F 18.998	N 14.007	H 1.0079	C 12.011	Li 6.941	B 10.811	O 15.999	Be 9.0122
Be 9.0122	He 4.0026	Li 6.941	F 18.998	H 1.0079	O 15.999	C 12.011	N 14.007	B 10.811
N 14.007	C 12.011	H 1.0079	Li 6.941	He 4.0026	B 10.811	Be 9.0122	F 18.998	O 15.999
F 18.998	B 10.811	O 15.999	N 14.007	Be 9.0122	C 12.011	Li 6.941	He 4.0026	H 1.0079

P. 235

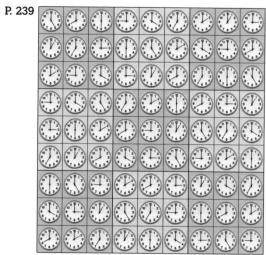

P. 236

GHI	TUV	PQRS	DEF	#★	JKL	MNO	WXYZ	ABC
DEF	#★	MNO	PQRS	WXYZ	ABC	JKL	TUV	GHI
JKL	WXYZ	ABC	TUV	MNO	GHI	DEF	#★	PQRS
TUV	JKL	WXYZ	GHI	ABC	MNO	PQRS	DEF	#★
#★	MNO	DEF	WXYZ	TUV	PQRS	GHI	ABC	JKL
PQRS	ABC	GHI	#★	JKL	DEF	WXYZ	MNO	TUV
WXYZ	DEF	TUV	JKL	PQRS	#★	ABC	GHI	MNO
MNO	PQRS	#★	ABC	GHI	WXYZ	TUV	JKL	DEF
ABC	GHI	JKL	MNO	DEF	TUV	#★	PQRS	WXYZ

P. 237

7	6	2	1	9	8	2	3	2
9	4	1	3	4	6	7	4	5
3	4	8	3	5	6	9	6	A
5	A	6	7	7	2	3	4	9
3	7	8	8	1	8	8	5	8
8	2	4	9	3	5	1	6	6
7	5	2	4	7	9	8	1	2
4	7	3	5	2	A	6	6	7
1	9	6	8	6	3	4	2	4

P. 238

三	五	一	七	六	四	八	二	九
六	九	七	二	八	五	三	四	一
二	四	八	九	一	三	六	七	五
八	二	五	一	四	九	七	六	三
一	三	九	六	七	二	四	五	八
七	六	四	五	三	八	九	一	二
九	七	三	四	二	一	五	八	六
四	八	二	三	五	六	一	九	七
五	一	六	八	九	七	二	三	四

P. 239

P. 240

VIII	III	IV	I	VI	IX	V	II	VII
VII	VI	IX	III	V	II	I	VIII	IV
I	V	II	VIII	IV	VII	VI	III	IX
IX	VII	I	V	II	VI	VIII	IV	III
V	II	III	IV	I	VIII	VII	IX	VI
IV	VIII	VI	IX	VII	III	II	I	V
III	IX	VII	VI	VIII	I	IV	V	II
VI	I	V	II	IX	IV	III	VII	VIII
II	IV	VIII	VII	III	V	IX	VI	I

P. 241

P. 242

P. 243

P. 244

P. 245

%	@	(	!	&	∧	#	$	⋆
∧	&	$	#	@	⋆	(	%	!
#	!	⋆	$	(	%	@	∧	&
$	(	!	@	∧	&	%	⋆	#
⋆	%	#	(	!	$	&	@	∧
&	∧	@	%	⋆	#	!	(	$
@	⋆	%	&	$	!	∧	#	(
!	#	∧	⋆	%	(	$	&	@
(	$	&	∧	#	@	⋆	!	%

SOLUTIONS

P. 246

N (14.007)	H (1.0079)	F (18.998)	B (10.811)	O (15.999)	He (4.0026)	C (12.011)	Be (9.0122)	Li (6.941)
O (15.999)	Be (9.0122)	C (12.011)	F (18.998)	Li (6.941)	N (14.007)	H (1.0079)	B (10.811)	He (4.0026)
B (10.811)	He (4.0026)	Li (6.941)	C (12.011)	H (1.0079)	Be (9.0122)	O (15.999)	F (18.998)	N (14.007)
C (12.011)	N (14.007)	Be (9.0122)	H (1.0079)	F (18.998)	O (15.999)	Li (6.941)	He (4.0026)	B (10.811)
H (1.0079)	O (15.999)	He (4.0026)	Be (9.0122)	B (10.811)	Li (6.941)	F (18.998)	N (14.007)	C (12.011)
F (18.998)	Li (6.941)	B (10.811)	He (4.0026)	N (14.007)	C (12.011)	Be (9.0122)	O (15.999)	H (1.0079)
Be (9.0122)	F (18.998)	N (14.007)	Li (6.941)	C (12.011)	B (10.811)	He (4.0026)	H (1.0079)	O (15.999)
He (4.0026)	C (12.011)	O (15.999)	N (14.007)	Be (9.0122)	H (1.0079)	B (10.811)	Li (6.941)	F (18.998)
Li (6.941)	B (10.811)	H (1.0079)	O (15.999)	He (4.0026)	F (18.998)	N (14.007)	C (12.011)	Be (9.0122)

P. 247

(Baseball-diamond grid solution)

P. 248

#★	TUV	MNO	WXYZ	PQRS	ABC	JKL	GHI	DEF
WXYZ	ABC	JKL	TUV	GHI	DEF	MNO	#★	PQRS
GHI	PQRS	DEF	JKL	MNO	#★	TUV	WXYZ	ABC
PQRS	DEF	#★	GHI	TUV	WXYZ	ABC	MNO	JKL
MNO	WXYZ	GHI	ABC	JKL	PQRS	#★	DEF	TUV
ABC	JKL	TUV	DEF	#★	MNO	WXYZ	PQRS	GHI
DEF	GHI	WXYZ	MNO	ABC	TUV	PQRS	JKL	#★
JKL	#★	ABC	PQRS	WXYZ	GHI	DEF	TUV	MNO
TUV	MNO	PQRS	#★	DEF	JKL	GHI	ABC	WXYZ

P. 249

(Sudoku solution with playing-card cells)

7	♠	5	6	4	3	2	8	9
♦	♦	4	8	7	♣	6	5	1
8	9	6	1	2	♠	♥	7	3
2	3	♠	♥	8	4	9	7	6
6	♥	♥	9	3	2	♥	♠	5
5	8	9	7	1	♦	♦	2	4
9	♥	♥	♠	6	1	4	3	7
1	7	3	♥	9	8	5	♠	2
4	6	2	3	5	7	1	♣	8

P. 250

八	四	二	六	一	三	五	九	七
一	五	三	七	二	九	六	八	四
六	七	九	四	五	八	一	三	二
七	三	八	二	四	五	九	六	一
二	六	四	三	九	一	七	五	八
五	九	一	八	七	六	四	二	三
四	二	五	九	八	七	三	一	六
三	一	七	五	六	二	八	四	九
九	八	六	一	三	四	二	七	五

P. 251

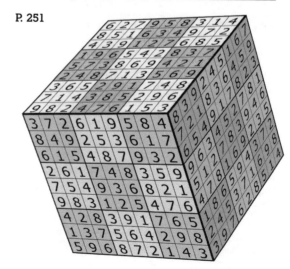

P. 252

P. 253

VIII	IV	III	II	VI	VII	I	IX	V
II	VII	I	IX	IV	V	VIII	VI	III
VI	V	IX	III	I	VIII	II	VII	IV
IX	VIII	V	VII	II	IV	VI	III	I
IV	III	II	I	IX	VI	V	VIII	VII
VII	I	VI	VIII	V	III	IV	II	IX
III	VI	VIII	V	VII	I	IX	IV	II
I	IX	IV	VI	III	II	VII	V	VIII
V	II	VII	IV	VIII	IX	III	I	VI

P. 254

▷ ABOUT THE AUTHORS

MAKI KAJI is the president and cofounder of the Japanese-based logic puzzle company, Nikoli Co. Ltd. Kaji is known as The Godfather of Sudoku, for establishing the modern rules of Sudoku and for giving the world-famous puzzle its name. Kaji started Nikoli in 1980.

The editors at **NIKOLI CO., LTD.** are the pioneers behind the first puzzle magazine in Japan, whose debut issue was published in August 1980, also called Nikoli. Since the first magazine in 1980, Nikoli has been publishing its own puzzle magazines and books, as well as supplying original puzzles to many newspapers and other weekly and monthly magazine publications throughout Japan and the world. The editors are constantly studying and inventing new puzzles and have created more than 250 original types of logic puzzles. Many of Nikoli's puzzles are handcrafted which makes the company one of a kind in the world. Once only known by Japanese puzzle solvers, but now celebrated worldwide, Nikoli stands for the best in handmade puzzles.

THE PUZZLES IN THIS COLLECTION WERE CREATED BY HAND BY THE FOLLOWING EDITORS:

Nob Kanamoto
Yu Sasaki
Nobuyuki Sakamoto
Kenichiro Yamano
Sumihiro Kobayashi
Takemasa Aoki

Yoshiyuki Watanabe
Takashi Kawasaki
Nobuki Kashihara
Yoshitaka Maeda
Daisuke Takei
Toshio Karino